FA
BIBLI

MW00604271

FACE-TO-FACE WITH

EUODIA AND SYNTYCHE

From CONFLICT *to* COMMUNITY

*Five Sessions for
Individuals, M&M'S (Mentors & Mentees, Friends, Family),
or Groups*

with

*Leader's Guide for Group-Study Facilitators,
and Session Guide*

JANET THOMPSON

NEW HOPE
PUBLISHERS
Birmingham, Alabama

New Hope® Publishers
P. O. Box 12065
Birmingham, AL 35202-2065
www.newhopepublishers.com
New Hope Publishers is a division of WMU®.

Library of Congress Cataloging-in-Publication Data

Thompson, Janet, 1947-

Face-to-face with Euodia and Syntyche : from conflict to community / Janet Thompson.

p. cm.

"5 sessions for individuals, M&M'S (mentors & mentees, friends, family) or groups with leader's guide for group study facilitators, and session guide."

Includes bibliographical references and index.

ISBN 978-1-59669-281-7 (sc : alk. paper) 1. Interpersonal conflict--Religious aspects--Christianity--Textbooks. 2. Interpersonal conflict--Biblical teaching--Textbooks. I. Title.

BV4597.53.C58T46 2009

220.8'3036--dc22

2009043828

ISBN-10: 1-59669-281-2
ISBN-13: 978-1-59669-281-7

N114125 • 0210 • 4M1

DEDICATED WITH LOVE

To

My husband, Dave,
who helped me learn to confront conflict.
My daughter Kim, who forgave as Jesus forgave her.
My Savior, Jesus Christ, the Prince of Peace.

TABLE OF CONTENTS

WELCOME

I began taking steps to start the Woman to Woman Mentoring Ministry while at my home church, Saddleback Church, in Lake Forest, California, pastored by Rick Warren. "Feed My sheep" was God's call and challenge to me to go into full-time ministry. God quickly revealed that *feeding* was mentoring and *the sheep* were women in churches all over the world. In obedience to the call, I launched the ministry in my home in January 1996, and we quickly outgrew my living room. After receiving numerous requests from other churches wanting to know how to start this type of a ministry, I authored *Woman to Woman Mentoring, How to Start, Grow, and Maintain A Mentoring Ministry DVD Leader Kit* (LifeWay Press).

As I traveled throughout the United States and Canada, training and speaking on mentoring, I heard numerous requests for a Bible study depicting God's plan for mentors and mentees — "M&M'S," as we fondly call them. One morning, as my husband completed his quiet time with the Lord, Dave asked me if I had ever considered writing Bible studies based on mentoring relationships in the Bible. He knew that many M&M'S enjoy doing a Bible study together, and Dave felt that one focused on what God says about mentoring relationships would help answer many of the M&M'S questions.

After much prayer—and my husband's prodding—I decided to look in the Bible to see how many mentoring relationships I could find. Before long, I had discovered 12. This was my confirmation to begin writing the "Face-to-Face" Bible study series (formerly known as *Mentoring God's Way*). My passion and life mission is to help one generation of believers connect to the next generation and pass down God's plan for the Christian life. I trust that the "Face-to-Face" Bible study series will help you do exactly that.

What Is Mentoring?

I love Dee Brestin's depiction of the informality of mentoring in *The Friendships of Women Workbook*: "It's not to be a dependent relationship, but simply a friendship as you spend time with a woman who is further down the road, at least in some areas of her Christian life. Win Couchman says, 'Mentoring works very nicely over a cup of coffee.'"

For those who like more concrete and specific definitions, *Roget's Super Thesaurus* provides this explanation of the root word of *mentoring*. It defines *mentor* as a teacher, guide, coach, or advisor. Most dictionaries define the word *mentor* as a trusted and wise counselor. To combine Dee's and the reference definitions with the Christian perspective: a Christian mentor is a spiritually mature woman who is a trusted and wise teacher, guide, coach, counselor, advisor, and friend. Thus, a *mentee* is someone willing to be taught, guided, coached, advised, or counseled by a trusted, wise, and spiritually older woman friend. Christian mentoring is sharing with another woman the many wonders you have seen God do in your life, and assuring her that He will do them in her life, too, as you both discover God's purpose and plan for your lives together.

Mentoring is not a hierarchy; it's always a two-way, mutually beneficial relationship where both participants learn from each other. Chris Tiegreen, author of my favorite devotional, *The One-Year Walk with God Devotional,* reminds us why it is always better to seek God's ways together.

> The Bible gives us solid wisdom on which to base our lives. But while it is absolute, its interpretation can vary widely. That's where advice comes in. Never underestimate the body of Christ. He has crafted us to live in community. Wisdom usually comes not to godly individuals but to godly fellowships. Are you seeking direction? Know your heart, but do not trust it entirely. Measure it by biblical wisdom and the counsel of those who follow it well.
> —June 27 devotional

The Bible also clearly instructs men to mentor men and women to mentor women. Titus 2:1–8 is the traditional "mentoring" passage.

> *You must teach what is in accord with sound doctrine. Teach the older men to be temperate, worthy of respect, self-controlled, and sound in faith, in love and in endurance. Likewise, teach the older*

women to be reverent in the way they live, not to be slanderers or addicted to much wine, but to teach what is good. Then they can train the younger women to love their husbands and children, to be self-controlled and pure, to be busy at home, to be kind, and to be subject to their husbands, so that no one will malign the word of God. Similarly, encourage the young men to be self-controlled. In everything set them an example by doing what is good. In your teaching show integrity, seriousness and soundness of speech that cannot be condemned, so that those who oppose you may be ashamed because they have nothing bad to say about us.

First Peter 5:2–4 (NLT) could be addressing mentors.

Care for the flock that God has entrusted to you. Watch over it willingly, not grudgingly—not for what you will get out of it, but because you are eager to serve God. Don't lord it over the people assigned to your care, but lead them by your own good example. And when the Great Shepherd appears, you will receive a crown of never-ending glory and honor.

A mentor doesn't need to be an expert on the Bible or God, and she doesn't need to have a perfect life. If that were the case, none of us would qualify. A mentor simply needs to be willing to share her life experiences with another woman and be an example and role model of how a Christian woman does life. And how do we learn to be a godly role model? Answer: *"Remember your leaders who taught you the word of God. Think of all the good that has come from their lives, and follow the example of their faith"* (Hebrews 13:7 NLT).

Mentoring is not *doing* a ministry: It is *being* a godly woman who follows the Lord's command: *"One generation will commend your works to another; they will tell of your mighty acts"* (Psalm 145:4).

WHO ARE M&M'S?

In the Woman to Woman Mentoring Ministry, we lovingly refer to mentors and mentees as "M&M'S"—no, that's not the candy, although we always have M&M's® candy at our events. And just like the candy, there are varieties of M&M relationships—no two are the same. M&M'S may be: friends, acquaintances, family members, workers, neighbors, members of a mentoring or other ministry, team members, women with similar life experiences, or any two women who want to grow spiritually together.

M&M'S AND MORE!

The "Face-to-Face" Bible study series has a variety of applications. You can enjoy this study in these ways:
- On your own
- As a mentor and mentee (M&M'S) in a mentoring or discipleship relationship
- Between two friends
- Between two relatives
- As a small or large group studying together
- As a churchwide Bible study

The Bible studies offer these three types of questions:
- On Your Own—questions for doing the study individually
- M&M'S—questions for mentors and mentees, two friends, or relatives studying together
- On Your Own and M&M'S—questions applicable to both individuals and those studying together
- Groups answer all the questions, with a Leader's/Facilitator's Guide in each book.

STUDY FORMAT

There are five main sessions, comprised of five study days. Each day's study includes:
- Scriptures and questions for you to study and answer
- Face-to-Face Reflections—a discussion of the day's topic

- Personal Parable—a story depicting and applying the day's topic
- Mentoring Moment—takeaway wisdom for the day

At the end of each session there is:
- Faith in Action—an opportunity for life application of the lessons learned
- Let's Pray Together—my prayer of agreement with you

Following session five are Closing Materials:
- Let's Pray a Closing Prayer Together
- Janet's Suggestions—ideas for further study
- Leader's Guide for Group-Study Facilitators and M&M'S
- Session Guide
- Prayer & Praise Journal

SUGGESTIONS FOR INDIVIDUAL STUDY

I admire you for seeking out this study on your own and having the desire and discipline to work on it by yourself. I like to grow in the knowledge of the Lord and His Word and have found that my most relevant insights from God come when I seek Him by myself in a quiet place. Have fun on your own, and share with someone all you are learning.

1. A good way to stay consistent in your studying is to work a little each day, during your quiet time in the morning or evening.

2. Tell someone you have started this study, and ask him or her to keep you accountable to complete it.

SUGGESTIONS FOR M&M'S— MENTORS AND MENTEES. FRIENDS. AND RELATIVES

I hope the study of *Face-to-Face with Euodia and Syntyche: From Conflict to Community* adds a new dimension to your M&M relationship.

Here are a few study tips:

1. Come to your meetings prepared to discuss your answers to the session's questions.

2. Or, you may decide to answer the questions together during your meetings.

3. If you don't live near each other, you can have phone or online discussions.

4. Remember, the questions are to enlighten and not divide; be honest and open as well as loving and kind.

SUGGESTIONS FOR GROUP STUDY

I love group studies because you get to hear other people's points of view, and lasting friendships often develop. Your meetings should be fun, informative, relevant, and applicable to group members' lives. Enjoy yourself with your fellow sisters in Christ, but remember that joining a group study *does* mean commitment. So please attend your scheduled meetings unless there is a real emergency. I suggest the following courtesies:

1. Put the meeting dates on your calendar.

2. Commit to doing your study and come prepared for the discussion. This honors the rest of the group, and you will get so much more from the sessions.

3. Ask questions—quite often, someone else has the same question.

4. Participate in the discussion, but be cautious of dominating the conversation. For example, if you have answered several questions, even though you know all the answers, let someone else have a turn. Try to encourage a less outgoing member to share.

5. Listen when others speak and give each speaker your full attention.

6. Arrive on time.

7. Keep in confidence the information shared in the group.

LEADERS AND FACILITATORS

When I lead and facilitate Bible-study groups, I value a complete and detailed Leader's Guide, so that is what I have provided for you. The "Face-to-Face" Bible study series has a Leader's Guide at the end of each book to provide the leader/facilitator with creative ideas for the following:

1. Guiding group discussion

2. Adding life application and variety to the sessions

3. Accommodating the varied learning styles of the group (visual learners, hands-on learners, auditory learners, and more)

TO YOU–THE READER

Whatever way you are doing this study, God has a message and a lesson just for you. Here are some suggestions I pray will enhance your experience studying *Face-to-Face with Euodia and Syntyche.*

1. Start each session with prayer and ask the Lord to speak to you through the Scripture readings, the prayerful answering of the questions, and the interaction with others.

2. Set your own pace. I provide breaking points, but make it comfortable for yourself and break as you need to do so.

3. If you're not sure how to answer a question, move on, but continue praying and thinking about the answer. Often my answers come quickly, but God's answers are the most fruitful.

Face-to-Face with Euodia and Syntyche

4. Unless otherwise indicated, all the questions relate to NIV Bible passages. Lists of Scriptures are sequential, as they appear in the Bible. You will be looking up Scripture references in your Bible—an invaluable way to study and learn about the Bible.

5. Use the space provided to answer questions, but don't feel obligated to fill the space. However, if you need more room, continue answering in a separate journal.

6. A book effectively used for study should be underlined, highlighted, and comments written in the margins, so interact with this material in that way.

7. At the end of session five, you will find suggestions from me on books to read or activities, to delve deeper into what God may be teaching you about the biblical M&M relationship featured in *Euodia and Syntyche*.

8. Use the Prayer & Praise Journal starting on page 139 to record the mighty work God does in your life during this study. Journal prayer requests, and note when God answers.

9. Have some chocolate. After reading about M&M'S throughout the study, you'll be ready for some candy!

My heart, admiration, and encouragement go out to you with this book. I pray that mentoring becomes a vital part of your life. The "Face-to-Face" Bible study series is another way the Lord allows me to "feed My sheep." And I hope that you will enjoy this and other "Face-to-Face" Bible studies and "feed" others as well.

About His Work,
Janet

THEIR STORY

CAN YOU RELATE?

BEAUTIFUL MUSIC BUT NO HARMONY

"The names 'Gilbert and Sullivan' are well known by all lovers of music. They produced 14 operas together in the period from 1871 to 1896. Gilbert's words allied with Sullivan's music produced magic.

The tragedy, however, is that the two men detested each other. The problem arose because Sullivan ordered some carpet for the theater they had bought, and when Gilbert saw the bill, he hit the roof. Neither could control his temper, and the two battled it out in court. They never spoke to one another again as long as they lived.

When Sullivan wrote the music for a new production, he mailed it to Gilbert. When Gilbert wrote the words, he mailed it back to Sullivan.

Once they were forced to be together during a curtain call, but they stood on opposite sides of the stage and bowed in different directions so they wouldn't see each other.

They knew how to make beautiful music, but they knew nothing about harmony." —Robert Morgan, *Nelson's Complete Book of Stories, Illustrations, & Quotes*

Day One

How Does Euodia and Syntyche's Story Relate to Us?

*O*nly two verses in the Bible refer to Euodia and Syntyche, and the women certainly don't have common names we readily recognize from Scripture or can easily pronounce. Yet we can learn a tremendous lesson about relationships and conflict resolution from these two succinct verses that the Apostle Paul wrote regarding these fellow ministry workers.

ON YOUR OWN AND M&M'S

Q: Read the Book of Philippians, focusing on 4:2–3.
• Considering Euodia and Syntyche's dispute might be the reason Paul wrote the letter to the Philippians, note verses in Philippians that could apply to resolving conflict.

Q: Read Acts 16:11–15, 40, which marks the beginning of the church at Philippi. It's likely Euodia and Syntyche were among the women who helped Lydia start the church. Compare the scene in these verses in Acts with the scene about 11 years later, in Philippians 4:2–3.

Q: How does Proverbs 18:19 apply to Gilbert and Sullivan, and Euodia and Syntyche?

Q: Describe an unresolved disagreement you've had, where the relationship ended.

- How did your unresolved dispute affect others?

Q: Now, describe a time when a disagreement was resolved and the friendship remained intact.

Q: What was the difference between the unresolved and resolved disputes?

M & M'S

Q: Make a commitment to each other to work though this study, keeping an open mind and a willingness to apply the principles you'll learn to your life and your current and future relationships.

FACE-TO-FACE REFLECTIONS

In the short passage in Philippians 4:2–3, we meet two Christian women who encountered conflict while serving in Paul's ministry in Philippi and who were unable to work out the problems on their own. They had not yet learned the art of agreeing to disagree.

Euodia and Syntyche probably were charter members of the church at Philippi. They worked with Paul as church planters and were influential women for him to mention them by name. Their argument was enough of an issue that he heard about it while under Roman imprisonment some 800 miles away. We can't minimize the significance of Paul addressing these women in a letter he knew would be read to the entire church publically, and quite possibly to surrounding churches. Arguments among Christians are a big deal!

Paul realized what a roadblock this divisive conflict would be to ministry and evangelism in Philippi—thus you'll see that the entire Book of Philippians addresses the conflict these women encountered and how to prevent conflict from disrupting the message of the Christian church.

When you compared your unresolved and resolved disputes, some of you might have said the difference was that in the unresolved scenario, you weren't yet a Christian, and in the resolved scenario, you were a believer with a softer, more compassionate heart. Others may feel that age and spiritual maturity assisted you in dealing with conflict, and still others might have read books or taken classes on anger management or dealing with life's disagreements. Still, there are many for whom this area of conflict continues to be a major struggle.

PERSONAL PARABLE

While writing this session, my phone rang. When I answered, I heard the sweet, southern voice of Cameron calling from a church that had a Woman to Woman Mentoring Ministry. Cameron shared that conflict was the theme of their last ministry event. I told her I was writing on that very subject and her phone call was a confirmation that the Lord wanted this Bible study written.

• • •

Mentoring Moment

"My mentor equipped me with ministry skills—but no one ever taught me to expect conflict. No one ever told me that every ministry leader experiences criticism, personal attacks, and church politics."—Sue Edwards, *Leading Women Who Wound*

• • •

Face-to-Face with Euodia and Syntyche

Day Two

Differences of Opinion Can Be Normal and Healthy

isagreements don't need to be fatal to a relationship; they do need recognition for what they are — differing viewpoints.

On Your Own and M&M's

Q: When are disagreements normal and healthy?

Q: Read 1 Corinthians 12:4–11. How do these verses reveal God's plan for each of us to have unique and different gifts and ideas?

- How are we to use our differences (v. 7)?

- What's the same in every believer's life, despite differences?

Q: Philippians 3:15 indicates Christians might think differently. Why don't all Christians have the same opinion?

Q: In what areas should mature Christians think the same (Philippians 2:1–2, 3:12–15)?

- If someone thinks differently on spiritual issues, who will make clear her thinking (3:15*b*)?

- What spiritual knowledge are we responsible to live by (3:16)?

- How do we mature spiritually (3:17)?

Q: How can a difference of opinion result in progress and positive change (Proverbs 27:17)?

Q: What terms describe a "healthy disagreement"?

Q: Are you good at fair debating or do you always have to win?

- Can you debate without arguing or becoming defensive? Explain.

ON YOUR OWN

Q: Who in your life depicts Proverbs 27:17, and how do they help you consider a different perspective than your viewpoint?

Q: To whom are you a sounding board; whose iron are you sharpening?

M & M'S

Q: How do you react when you have differing opinions?

Q: What are ways you give each other freedom to disagree?

Q: How does Proverbs 27:17 apply to your relationship?

Q: Mentor, take note of Philippians 3:17. Your role is helping your mentee to mature spiritually. She's looking to you to be an example and role model.

God made us each unique, with different gifts and points of view. That's healthy! Differing opinions bring breakthroughs.

We should allow others to express opinions that differ from ours and consider their merit. We don't have to *accept* a contrasting opinion, but we should graciously *acknowledge* it. We can then defend our original point of view, rethink it, or expand on it.

Fair debate or discussion is a healthy way to express or acknowledge a differing opinion. We see debates every election season. Speech classes teach acceptable debate techniques. Unfortunately, most of us have *disputes* instead of *debates*. When challenged, we want to prove our point and win, sometimes at any cost—not becoming behavior for a Christian. Only God can change another person's heart. Paul reminds us that the fundamentals of Christian faith are not debatable.

Personal Parable

My daughter Kim and her husband, Toby, attend Eagle Christian Church in Idaho, pastored by Dr. Steven A. Crane. The church mission statement epitomizes healthy Christian agreement and disagreement: "We have made it our mission as a church that we will be unified in essentials. We want to give liberty and grace in the non-essentials, and to love God's way in everything. We want to be a place of truth and a place of love."

Summarized: Essentials—Unity. Nonessentials— Liberty. In all things—Love!

Mentoring Moment

"What makes a relationship work is having things in common. What makes a relationship passionate are our differences."—Anonymous

DAY THREE

WHEN ARE DIFFERENCES OF
OPINION UNHEALTHY?

*I*n *Leading Women Who Wound*, author Susan Edwards admits, "No one ever told me to expect personal attacks and conflict when serving the Lord and Christians... I was naïve. And I was ignorant. I had never been taught strategies to manage conflict, so I did not always respond wisely."

ON YOUR OWN AND M&M'S

Q: It's unhealthy when differences of opinion cause division among believers (1 Corinthians 3:3–9). What did the Apostle Paul remind the Corinthians in verse 9?

Q: What does each verse warn about divisiveness among Christians?
- Matthew 12:25
- Romans 16:17–19
- 1 Corinthians 11:17–19
- 1 Corinthians 12:25–26
- Titus 3:10–11
- Hebrews 4:12

Q: In 1 Corinthians 1:10–13, what does it mean to have *"no division"* among us? To what does division lead? Who is never divided?

Q: What church circumstances offer fertile ground for division?

Q: Why do *all* relationships provide the perfect opportunity for conflicts or disagreements?

Q: Read Luke 11:17. Do you have division with other believers on any issues? Explain.

● Would you characterize this disagreement as healthy or unhealthy? Give reasons for your answer.

Q: How could doing this study help prevent your "house," or ministry, from falling?

Q: What could cause division between a Christian and her family or friends (Luke 12:51)?

● Have you personally experienced this type of division?

Q: Believers don't need *unanimity* in everything, but do need *unity* in working for the Lord. What does this statement mean to you?

M & M'S

Q: Have you (or are you now) experiencing an unhealthy or healthy disagreement in your relationship? If so, how are you going to resolve the issue to the glory of God?

FACE-TO-FACE REFLECTIONS

There's a misconception that Christians always agree. But church splits have occurred since Christianity's beginning because humans are imperfect. Many churches divide over questions like—pews or chairs? Traditional or contemporary music? Rebuild or refurbish?

While these issues may seem petty, people often marry so strongly to their opinions that they won't budge. That's unhealthy; it's debate gone bad.

An ad in a magazine caught my attention. A caption next to a man on his knees praying read: "Even when they disagree, Christians should share the same position." Below the picture, it read: "Where there's disagreement, there's reason for prayer. Because in the humble search for God's answers we find understanding. So before you take a stand for what you believe, spend some time on your knees."

PERSONAL PARABLE

When I first started the Woman to Woman Mentoring Ministry, I expected all Christians serving in ministry to get along and agree. The first time there was a major conflict among the women serving, I was shocked. I wasn't prepared to deal with the ensuing disruption compromising ministry work.

Some of the divisive disagreements were issues with each other and some were issues with me. I was observing Christian women who didn't know how to fight fair; they weren't living the scriptural foundations of the ministry.

While it was a rude awakening to discover that even Christian women have disagreements, I knew the key to peaceful relationships was learning how to biblically work through differences and not let them escalate into divisive arguments. Philippians 4:2–3 came alive to me.

If the mentoring ministry was going to survive, we needed to restore the spiritual health of the team. We had to move from conflict to community.

Mentoring Moment

"I have never yet known the Spirit of God to work where the Lord's people were divided." —D. L. Moody

Face-to-Face with Euodia and Syntyche

DAY FOUR

CONFLICT AVOIDANCE

"*A*ccording to a 1990 Gallup Mirror of America survey, most Americans avoid clashes with their friends. When asked, 'Do you ever get into serious arguments with your friends?' only 13 percent said yes. Eighty percent gave a resounding no, indicating that they failed to challenge the relationship by discussing negative feelings." — Brenda Hunter, *In the Company of Women*

ON YOUR OWN AND M&M'S

Q: Paul wasn't afraid to confront conflict. Philippians 3:1 may imply this wasn't his first correspondence with the Philippians on the issues he brings up in this letter. Why does Paul take the time to write to them again (v. 3:1*b*)?

Q: Paul wrote two letters to many of the churches. First Corinthians addresses immorality in that church. Read 2 Corinthians 7:8–13. What were the rewards of Paul's willingness to confront the Corinthians, even though the letter was painful for them?

Q: Not every confrontation must result in conflict. Read 2 Timothy 2:25–26. What was Paul's advice to young pastor Timothy regarding how to approach people?

Q: What should be our attitude when we confront someone?
- Ephesians 4:15   • Philippians 2:5   • 1 Peter 2:17

Q: What terms and applications for the word *confront* don't indicate conflict? For example, *Face-to-Face* is a term, and *I confronted my weight issue* is an application. Can you think of others?

Q: How should we receive wise counsel or justifiable criticism (Proverbs 13:10 and 15:31–33)?

Q: Based on Paul's letter to the church at Philippi, do you think Euodia and Syntyche were confronting their conflict issues? Why or why not?

Q: Why do most women avoid conflict?
- Give examples of ways women avoid conflict:

Q: How do you typically handle conflict?

Q: If you're one of the few people who enjoy a good debate, how do you avoid the discussion escalating to an angry exchange?

Q: Describe a potential conflict you recently encountered.

- Did you confront the issue with the person or avoid it?
- Are you satisfied with the way you acted?
- Were you happy with the outcome? Explain.

Q: Have you *knowingly* wronged or hurt someone and then been afraid or reluctant to face the person? Explain:

Q: When have you felt God nudging you to face or confront an issue from your past, and what helped you deal with this issue?

- If you still avoid the issue, what would help you confront it now?

Face-to-Face with Euodia and Syntyche

M & M'S

Q: Take a moment to evaluate how you both typically handle a conflict; confront or avoid?
- Discuss the value of respectfully confronting in love.
- Mentor, share tips for successfully confronting conflict.

Q: Are there difficult issues in your mentoring relationship that you haven't confronted and you feel ready to face now?

Q: You're in a close relationship—fertile ground for misunderstandings and misspoken words. Discuss ways to let the other person know you are offended.

- Mentor, like Paul, your role as the spiritually mature M&M is to confront any spiritual or moral issues your mentee might be struggling with in her life; and you may need to confront these issues more than once.
- Mentee, be receptive to your mentor's wise counsel. She wants to help you mature in your Christian faith.

FACE-TO-FACE REFLECTIONS

Fear and self-preservation are at the heart of most conflict avoidance. We fear rejection, alienation, hurting the other person's feelings, or dealing with her reaction—what if she gets angry, defensive, cries, or goes ballistic? Or what if *we* cry, are speechless, or lose control?

We fear picking an appropriate time to confront, or don't want to admit we're wrong. We doubt our feelings are justified and minimize or avoid the problem, hoping it will go away. Rather than overcoming our fears or pride, we may actually end a relationship.

Conflict is inevitable, and can be healthy, if we work through and grow from it. Resolving disagreements should create *cohesiveness*, not *divisiveness*.

Confrontation doesn't have to result in conflict. The problem usually arises with the way we challenge and confront, or fail to confront. Brenda Hunter poses the question in her book, *In the Company of Women*, "Why can't women use their considerable social skills to solve problems in friendships?" Then she quotes writer Sherryl Kleinman's answer: "We [women] want 'peaceable relationships' that we can idealize."

But Hunter also warns: "When a friend hurts us or ignores us, we begin an inner dialogue. We begin unconsciously to exonerate ourselves and devalue our friend. We tell ourselves how wronged we were and how insensitive our friend is. And the longer we refuse to address the wall between us, the more we fester and withdraw. In the end, our self-righteousness destroys any possibility of reconciliation."

PERSONAL PARABLE

I relate to Kleinman's statement about idealizing relationships. I want everyone to get along and be happy in our ministry and family, and I don't like confrontation or conflict. But there is conflict in life—especially when women are serving together—and it may be up to *me* to confront the issues. So, I remind myself to stop and pray about when to bring up an issue and how to convey my message in love.

God recently let me practice my confrontation skills. My neighbors were not at home and their dogs were barking nonstop. It was frustrating me. God answered my prayer about how and when to talk with my wonderful neighbor, in a way that reflected His love. As we were returning home from a walk together, the dogs were barking. I seized the perfect opportunity to discuss the noisiness in her absence. I empathized by saying that I understood she would not have known about it. She was grateful I spoke up and informed her. My honesty and her receptiveness strengthened our relationship.

* * *

Mentoring Moment

"Women need direction on how to manage conflict
with other *women*."—Sue Edwards, *Leading Women Who Wound*

* * *

Face-to-Face with Euodia and Syntyche

DAY FIVE

CONSEQUENCES OF
UNRESOLVED CONFLICT

From Paul's double plea to Euodia and Syntyche, we ascertain the two women had an equal role in an ongoing feud. Since Paul included the conflict of Euodia and Syntyche in his letter to the Philippians, and even asked others to intervene, we can assume the two women weren't working out the problem on their own. The women had ministered beside Paul, probably helping plant the church at Philippi—and were still involved and prominent in the ministry of winning souls for Christ—Paul's main mission. It was essential to the ministry in Philippi that Euodia and Syntyche reach a resolution to their disagreement.

ON YOUR OWN AND M&M'S

Q: Why did Paul use the word *plead* twice in Philippians 4:3?

Q: Read Philippians 1:3–6, 2:12–16, 4:3. What was the ministry of Paul, Euodia and Syntyche, and the Philippians?

Q: How should servants of the Lord spreading the gospel behave (Philippians 1:27–28 and 2 Timothy 2:22–24)?

Q: What negative consequences could occur from Euodia and Syntyche's public unresolved conflict and how might it affect
- the church congregation?

- the surrounding community?

- their witness for Christ?

- Paul's ministry?

Q: Likewise, in 1 Corinthians 3:1–3, Paul scolds the Corinthian church for their conflict issues. What does he call them (v. 1) and what are they acting like (v. 3)?

- What distinguishes the spiritually mature (Hebrews 5:12–14)?

- What grieves Paul regarding the consequences of their quarrelling and fighting (2 Corinthians 12:20–21)?

Q: Read Galatians 5:19–21. List the acts of the sinful nature.

- Which ones apply to conflict?

- Does Paul differentiate any sins as worse than the others?

- What is the sinful nature in conflict with (vv. 16–18)?

- What consequences does Paul warn against (v. 21*b*)?

Q: What counters the sinful nature's acts (Galatians 5:22–26)?

- How has the fruit of the Spirit helped you *"crucify your sinful nature"* (v. 24) and *"keep in step with the Spirit"* (v. 25)?

Q: What negative consequences have you encountered from unresolved conflict in your life, ministry, church, or community?

Face-to-Face with Euodia and Syntyche

Galatians 5:24 says, *"Those who belong to Christ Jesus."* Have you made a commitment to accept and follow Jesus as your personal Savior? If not, would you like to do so right now? If you're ready, go to the Face-to-Face Reflections and sincerely pray the Salvation Prayer on page 32. You're immediately welcomed into the family of God and the community of believers. Congratulations!

If you have questions about becoming a Christian, talk to a Christian friend or pastor who can help you find the answers. Much of what we talk about in this study will seem foreign to an unbeliever—like loving and forgiving the person who wronged you. None of us can forgive without Jesus and the Holy Spirit's power.

M & M'S

Q: Discuss negative consequences of any unresolved conflict in each of your lives.

● What skills in conflict resolution do you both need to learn?

Q: Mentee, if you haven't accepted Jesus into your heart and would like to do so right now, go to the Salvation Prayer in the Face-to-Face Reflections on page 32 and sincerely pray with your mentor. Or pray alone, though your mentor would love being with you as you receive Jesus as your personal Savior and celebrate together your entry into the family of God!

● If you still have questions about becoming a Christian, talk to your mentor, or a pastor who can give you the assurance you seek. You won't be able to do what we talk about in this study on your own. Only Jesus and the Holy Spirit can give us a heart that completely forgives those who hurt us.

FACE-TO-FACE REFLECTIONS

Often talking through an issue can result in a resolution or truce. However, a major cause of women's unresolved conflict is the "stuffing" of negative feelings. We paint a fake, tense smile across our face, but inside we're seething. The consequence: a destructive external bitter eruption, or a harbored internal bitter root.

A second cause of unresolved conflict is avoidance. We make elaborate excuses not to spend time with the person we're upset with or we boycott places where she'll be present. We don't go to a meeting or Bible study, or if we do, we avoid eye contact and sit a distance from her—maybe even pretending she's not there. We're coolly polite and physically present, but our heart and spirit are elsewhere. The consequence: a broken relationship.

A third cause of unresolved conflict is not confronting the other person. We tell everyone else about the problem, except the person with whom we have the issue. Maybe we hope others will tell her for us or we want to download our problem onto someone else hoping they'll side with us. The consequence: we indulge in the sin of gossip and slander.

None of these consequences is appropriate for Christ followers. God has provided healthy ways to resolve conflict and avoid the negative consequences of unresolved conflict.

If any of you haven't made a commitment to follow God and accept Jesus as personal Savior, pray sincerely this salvation prayer.

Salvation Prayer

Dear God, I know I have a sinful nature, and I have given into that sin many times. I have grieved You, and Your ways have not been my ways. Today, I want to change my life by asking Your forgiveness for my past sins, and with help from the Holy Spirit, I want to turn from my sinful ways and live a changed life in the future. I know I don't deserve forgiveness, but I believe You sent Your only Son, Jesus Christ, to die on the Cross for my sins, and He rose again three days later. I believe You'll forgive me and grant me eternal life. Thank You, Jesus! Help me to cast off my old way of doing things and learn how to live a new life that is pleasing to You. And let it start today! Amen.

Face-to-Face with Euodia and Syntyche

Linda LeSourd Lader shares in *In the Company of Women* how, after becoming a Christian in her 20s, she learned to avoid the negative consequences of conflict in female friendships while living with a group of women. "That's when I developed friendships where there was a real commitment to each other and…said there would be no back door in our friendships. If you lock the door in a friendship, you know you can't run from problems and misunderstandings and you have to find a way to work them out."

Mentoring Moment

"Conflicts are turned into opportunities for people to be freed from sin and mature in faith and character."
—Ken Sande, President, Peacemaker Ministries

FAITH IN ACTION

What one thing from this session does God want you to apply?

LET'S PRAY TOGETHER

Lord, we know how important it is for Christians to get along, and yet it's so difficult to confront and deal with conflict. Help us approach each other in love and learn ways of resolving our disagreements in a manner pleasing to You. And Lord, help us share what we learn with other Christian brothers and sisters tangled in the web of anger and bitterness that gives Satan a foothold into our lives. Let us learn to love others as You love them. Amen.

THE ROOT
OF CONFLICT

Day One

What Do We Fight About?

onflict rears its disruptive head in all kinds of circumstances and invades all our relationships. Understanding why we're upset is the key to resolving potentially destructive conflict.

On Your Own and M&M's

Q: Considering that Euodia and Syntyche were evangelists spreading the good news in Philippi and working in the church, speculate regarding what they may have been arguing about.

• What do you think was at the root of their issues?

Q: Read James 4:1–5. Why does James say we have conflict?

Q: Read Romans 12:4–8. How could conflict result from having our own God-given purpose?

• Why does God give each of us a different purpose and what are we to do with it (Philippians 2:13)?

Q: What does Romans 12:3 warn about keeping our purpose in perspective?

• Whose purpose should prevail (Philippians 2:13)?

M&M'S

Q: Discuss the purpose God has given each of you and how this might be a source of conflict between you.
• What can you do to ensure that your uniqueness strengthens rather than divides your relationship?

FACE-TO-FACE REFLECTIONS

Did you arrive at pride, a self-righteous attitude, poor communication skills, personality differences, and spiritual immaturity as possible root causes of conflict between Euodia and Syntyche? These are the same causes of conflict among women today.

Perhaps Euodia or Syntyche thought Paul favored the other one and chose her more often to work with him. They could have argued over the "right way" to do ministry. Or maybe who should have the most platform time or get to lead the sinner's prayer. Maybe Paul wrote the word *plead* twice—*I plead with Euodia and I plead with Syntyche*—so they wouldn't argue about him blaming or giving top billing to one more than the other.

At the root of most of our "differences" is God's intention to make each of us different from the next. Perhaps Euodia and Syntyche had completely different personalities and spiritual gifts. I see Euodia as a free-spirit gathering people for a time of joyful worship where the Holy Spirit, in His time, would move and save lives. Spreading the good news should be *fun!*

With a name like Syntyche, maybe she was a "techie," a stickler for details. Or perhaps she was an aggressive, task-oriented, bossy leader-type, who kept doing Euodia's job before Euodia could get to it. Spreading the good news should be *orderly* and *organized.*

Face-to-Face with Euodia and Syntyche

Both women wanted to serve the Lord and share the gospel, but they differed on the way to accomplish that goal, and neither was willing to compromise or bend.

PERSONAL PARABLE

I can relate to different styles of ministry and personality when my friend Jane and I do training conferences together. While introducing us, Jane points out that I'm the organized, detail-oriented one, and she's not. Jane likes a lively atmosphere, and the most important thing for her is that participants enjoy themselves!

Preparing a training room, I focus on having the correct handouts, an adjustable podium, and setting up my book table—logistical things. Jane is busy decorating the tables and selecting background music—fun things!

Once we spoke on the Fourth of July and Jane insisted we wear red, white, and blue. She brought flag table runners: red, white, and blue M&M's; glitter; and handmade flag bead pens for the audience. From the podium I watched ladies brushing glitter off their handouts, but I also saw the joy on Jane and their faces as they munched M&M's.

Jane further explains that through her and my many differences of personality, age, spiritual maturity, and season of life, she has learned that women can serve in ministry and complement each other—with Christ at the center. The best compliment is when someone tells us that, in spite of our differences, we're a good team together.

Mentoring Moment

God made us diverse, but often diversity is what divides us.

Day Two

I Want My Own Way

et's take a closer look at two intertwining roots of conflict: pride and jealousy. The Bible has much to say about these two sins because the Lord knew we would each wage a personal battle with Satan, who is ready to use our ego to disrupt relationships. Satan knows our Achilles heal: we want to be right, and we want what isn't ours.

On Your Own and M&M's

Q: We discussed in session one that *fear* is often the reason we avoid confrontations. What are we afraid of?

- What's at the core of those fears?
- What's at the center of wanting our own way?

Q: Who does pride edge out (Psalm 10:4)?

Q: How does God feel about pride?
- Proverbs 8:13
- Proverbs 16:18
- Obadiah 1:3–4
- James 4:6

Q: Define pride in your own words.

- How can you counter pride (Philippians 2:3–8)?

Q: What antidote to pride does 1 Peter 5:5–6 confirm?
● How do you develop this (James 3:13, 4:10)?

● What results from pride, rather than humility (Proverbs 11:2)?

● Who seeks to keep you from becoming humble (1 Peter 5:8–9)?

Q: Read Matthew 4:1–11. How did Satan try to tempt Jesus?

● How did Jesus resist Satan (Ephesians 6:17)?

Q: How can you resist Satan (Ephesians 6:10–18)?

Q: Read Philippians 2:5–11. Who is our role model of humility?

Q: A result of untamed pride is jealousy; we think we deserve what others have. Read Genesis 37:1–4, 11–22, 26–28, 36. Discuss how jealousy devastates relationships.

Q: Joseph's brothers wanted their father to love them as much as he loved Joseph. What does one of the Ten Commandments warn about wanting what others have (Deuteronomy 5:21)?

● Coveting is another form of jealousy. How can you overcome jealousy and coveting (Romans 13:8–10; Galatians 6:4)?

Q: What wise counsel does the Bible give about avoiding the entanglements of jealousy, coveting, and envy?
● Proverbs 14:30   ● James 3:13–16
● Ecclesiastes 4:4   ● 1 Peter 2:1
● Galatians 5:25–26

Q: Describe a team project you participated in where people's insistence on doing things their own way resulted in division and incompletion of the task. If you were the one wanting your own way, how do you feel about that now?

Q: Envying God's calling on another woman's life can derail your own calling. How can you prevent this in your life and ministry?

Q: How has today's lesson encouraged you to be happy for others' success and be satisfied with what God has given you?

Q: If you struggle with wanting your own way, or wanting what others have, personalize and pray Matthew 6:10 every morning. *"May Your kingdom come, Your will, not _____'s will, be done in my life today as it is in heaven."*

ON YOUR OWN

Q: Search your heart before you answer this question: do you struggle with wanting your own way or wanting what someone else has? If so, write a confession to God here:

Q: Personalize and pray today's Scriptures by inserting your name. Choose several to memorize.

Q: If you don't have an accountability partner, ask someone to assume that role in helping you apply what you learn in this study.

M & M'S

Q: If either of you admit to wanting things your way and/or struggling with jealousy and coveting, confess that sin and pray for each other.

Q: Accountability partners help each other apply what they commit to change. Allow each other to assume that role in your relationship, and establish mutually agreeable guidelines. Usually the mentor keeps the mentee accountable; but mentor, you may find this study challenges you to make some changes where you would like accountability also.

Q: Personalize and pray today's Scriptures together. Choose several to memorize and keep each other accountable.

Face-to-Face Reflections

It breaks my heart when women forget we're on the same side. Instead of uniting, we divide; and so often, our division results from wanting to do things our own way. We aren't tolerant of others' ideas and suggestions.

Some of our problems stem from not knowing how to communicate our ideas in a kind and loving way without offending the other person. Or pride and ego are the seeds of conflict. We want our name on the project, or we're jealous of the person who gets applause and recognition instead of being happy we're on her team.

We live in a world that says, "It's all about you!" But Christian women aren't of this world. We're of the world of Jesus Christ, who humbled Himself on the Cross to give undeserving, lowly us the guarantee of eternal life. Yet often we act like deserving gods. Satan knows he can get to us with his weapon of pride. We're especially vulnerable if we're a new believer or serving in ministry.

Tied to pride are jealousy, envy, and coveting. Our pride tells us, *You deserve it!* And when we don't have *it*, we often try to take down the person who does, or we're secretly joyful when she suffers loss.

I was reading the Easter story to my toddler grandchildren out of *The Beginner's Bible*. One of the story lines is: "The leaders in Jerusalem did not like Jesus. They saw how many people were following him, and they were angry about it." I would pause, and my three-year-old granddaughter, Katelyn, would scowl and fill in the next words, "They were *jealous*!"

Then the kids and I read the story of Joseph and his brothers, "Jacob made Joseph a colorful robe." Again, Katelyn knew the next words, "His brothers were *jealous*."

The Bible warns that, "*The human heart is the most deceitful of all things, and desperately wicked. Who really knows how bad it is? But I, the LORD, search all hearts and examine secret motives. I give all people their due rewards, according to what their actions deserve*" (Jeremiah 17:9–10 NLT).

I was having breakfast with my fellow women's leadership trainers when the men's ministry leader joined us. He commented that men and women do ministry differently: "Women share openly together eye-to-eye, knee-to-knee." Then, putting the saltshaker in the center of the table, he said, "Let's say the saltshaker is the goal. Men move side-by-side, shoulder-to-shoulder toward the goal, ministry happens, and relationships develop."

The trainers reflected that even though women do better at one-on-one relationships, men outdo us in uniting for a purpose: working as teammates. We also concluded that pride and resultant lack of unity caused division or splits in teams, relationships, and congregations.

One trainer said she saw an example of this at her church: "The home-schooling moms are separating from the public-school moms and the working moms feel alienated from the stay-at-home moms."

Instead of reaching out in love and working side-by-side for the common goal of raising godly children in the same church, community, and family of God—they divide and split.

Mentoring Moment

"It's not about you." — Rick Warren, *The Purpose Driven Life*

"When you get your own way, you nurse a hideous idol called self. But when you give up your way, you get God." — Janet Erskin Stewart, *The One Year with God Devotional*, June 6

Face-to-Face with Euodia and Syntyche

DAY THREE

YOU MAKE ME SO ANGRY!

nger can be a *root* and a *result* of conflict; and left to fester, it opens the door for potential sin. Anger isn't necessarily a sin, but *staying* angry can lead to sin.

ON YOUR OWN AND M&M'S

Q: What do the following verses say about anger?
- Proverbs 15:18
- Proverbs 22:24–25
- Proverbs 29:11, 22
- Proverbs 30:33
- Ecclesiastes 7:9
- James 1:19–20

Q: Read about Jesus's display of righteous anger in John 2:12–16. List situations where anger would be an appropriate emotion.

Q: Read Ephesians 4:26–27. Verse 26 recognizes we'll experience the emotion of anger. But Euodia and Syntyche's rift had lasted long enough for Paul to hear about it while imprisoned far away, and for his letter to travel a great distance to Philippi! What sins can result from harboring the anger of unresolved conflict?

Q: Did you mention bitterness? What does the Bible warn about the root of bitterness?
- Job 21:22–26
- Proverbs 14:10
- Acts 8:21–23
- James 3:14–15

Q: How does Ephesians 4:31–32 tell us to counter bitterness, rage, anger, brawling, and slander?

Q: After you read today's Face-to-Face Reflections, return and answer these questions.
- Are you an "outie" or an "inie"?
- What is the best balance of the two?

Q: Are you harboring anger toward someone? Explain.

- Has the anger turned to bitterness? What could you do to rid yourself of that bitterroot?

ON YOUR OWN

Q: As you work through this study, commit to putting into practice what you learn.

Q: Have you found an accountability partner or mentor yet? The Christian life is easier with someone cheering you on.

M & M'S

Q: Mentor, be sure your mentee understands how anger can become sin. Commit to helping each other put into practice what you are learning.

Q: If either of you are angry with someone, keep each other accountable to the ABCD steps on page 45.

Face-to-Face with Euodia and Syntyche

Jesus experienced anger, and because we're made in His image, we'll experience it too. There is a time for justifiable, righteous anger, but where we go wrong is letting our anger turn vengeful and allowing anger to escalate to harming ourselves or someone else. Then anger becomes sin.

Anger is an emotion felt in the moment that requires quick resolution. You cannot retrieve actions or words. Many horrific acts occur and hateful words are hurled in a "fit of anger." Uncontrolled, raging anger is unacceptable.

Doug Fields, a former pastor at Saddleback church, likes to describe anger in terms of "outies" and "inies." An "outie" is someone who spews out anger, not holding anything back, and then is ready to move on. The problem is the potential for people to be hurt during the verbal—and maybe even physical—outburst.

"Inies" are the ones who profess they aren't mad. "Everything's fine," they say, while anger churns inside, turning into bitterness. "Inies" find quiet, sly, unexpected ways to express their anger, or some never let go of anger—they take it to the grave. Other "inies" can hold their anger inside only so long before the pressure builds into a sudden and violent eruption—the fallout being lethal to themselves and anyone in their vicinity.

So how do you have *healthy* anger? Here are some ABCD steps to consider practicing:

Acknowledge — You're angry. Admit it.

Breathe — Take a timeout and step away from the source of anger. Breathe deeply.

Call on God — He knows what you should do regarding the source of your anger—ask Him.

Defuse — Release your anger to God.

I know well the toll anger and bitterness can take on a person and everyone in the angry person's life. My family experienced a terrible, life-altering tragedy when I was ten years old. My father was a highway patrol officer, shot with his own gun while on duty. He died instantly, just a week before his 37th birthday. Prior to my father's death, my mother was a Sunday School teacher. But she blamed God for my father's murder, and to her dying day, she was angry with God, and often, with the rest of the world. That intense anger turned to bitterness and an obsessive need to control everything and everyone.

My mother never turned back to God for the comfort and solace she so desperately needed, and I watched the bitterness eat away at her spiritually, emotionally, and physically. At the end of her life, she had alienated everyone who loved her. It's painful remembering her lonely hermit life and her refusal to allow God's love to replace her lost love.

● ● ●

Mentoring Moment

"Emotions are meant to be *instructive* not *destructive*."
—Pastor Tom Holladay, *The Relationship Lessons of Jesus*

*"Some men stay happy till the day they die . . .
others have no happiness at all;
they live and die with bitter hearts"*
(Job 21:23–25 GNT).

● ● ●

Face-to-Face with Euodia and Syntyche

DAY FOUR

HAVE YOU HEARD?

*I*n the midst of conflict, we want our voice heard, whether it's justifying or defending our position, telling our side of the story, or expressing our unhappiness with the situation. Unfortunately, that intense desire to speak our *piece* disrupts *peace* if we cross the line and speak to anyone who will listen.

ON YOUR OWN AND M&M'S

Q: It's likely Euodia and Syntyche exchanged angry or harsh words. We often fail to appreciate the power of our words. Read James 3:2–12.

- Why do we all struggle with misspoken words (v. 2)?

- What is the paradox James describes in verses 9–12?

Q: Note the respect for words each of these verses commands:
- Psalm 59:12
- Proverbs 12:18
- Proverbs 15:1–2
- Proverbs 18:6–7,21
- Proverbs 21:23
- Matthew 12:36–37

Q: Where does our propensity for speaking unrighteous words start?
- Job 36:13
- Psalm 17:10
- Proverbs 10:20
- Jeremiah 9:8
- Matthew 12:34–35
- Matthew 15:18–19
- Mark 7:20–23

Q: How can we change our hearts (Psalm 119:11)?

Q: Who knows what we're going to say before we say it (Psalm 139:4)?
- What should we do before we speak (Proverbs 15:28)?

- What can you do to remind yourself to do this?

Q: Mother Teresa once said, "Kind words can be short and easy to speak, but their echoes are truly endless." What does God's Word say about the words He wants us speaking?
- Psalm 119:13
- Proverbs 16:13, 21, 23–24
- Ephesians 4:25,29
- Colossians 4:6

Q: Euodia and Syntyche might have talked to others about their side of the conflict. What does 1 Timothy 5:13 call that behavior?
- What does gossip do to relationships (Proverbs 16:28)?

- How does gossip start or fuel conflict (Proverbs 26:20–22)?

Q: Solomon had much to say about the sin of gossip. Note the advice or warning each verse provides:
- Proverbs 10:19
- Proverbs 11:9, 12–13
- Proverbs 20:19
- Proverbs 26:22

Q: What are some other terms for *gossip*?

Q: Define in your own words the term *slander*.

Q: Read Titus 2:3–5. What are we to teach the next generation about gossip and slander?

Q: If you slander someone, what does James 4:11–12 say you're doing?
- What do Matthew 7:1–5 and James 5:9 warn about judging others?

Q: What are ways to lovingly (Ephesians 4:15) let someone know they're gossiping or slandering?

Q: How can you avoid becoming an accomplice and listening to gossip (Psalm 28:3; Proverbs 29:24)?

Q: Where do Christians often gossip or slander while thinking they're doing a "spiritual good deed"?

Q: List key gossip words or trigger sentences. Next to them put a tactful counter comment or question to stop the gossip before hearing it and becoming an accomplice. See the example.

Trigger Gossip Words/Phrases	Lovingly Change the Subject
I just *heard* Mary needs prayer because…	Did Mary ask others to pray?

Q: Do your words usually build up or tear down?
- Do you squelch gossip or are you a spreader or accomplice?

- Are you critical or judgmental of others?
- If you're not pleased with your words, what will you do to change?

M & M'S

Q: This is a good time to review together Titus 2:3–5. Mentor, what can you teach to your mentee regarding gossip and slander?

Q: Mentee, write your questions about what constitutes slander or gossip and discuss with your mentor.

Q: How will you stop gossip and slander from invading your relationship? Make notes here:

FACE-TO-FACE REFLECTIONS

Words have power. They can crush spirits, annihilate reputations, start wars, spread lies, entice betrayal, spark jealousies, and inflict deep emotional wounds. Or they can raise spirits, enhance reputations, maintain peace, spread truth, create loyalty, encourage camaraderie, and soothe wounds. God meant words to be a blessing and Satan uses them for cursing. The Word of God and prayer help us to discern the difference.

Women love to talk. The more we do, we expose what's in our heart. To change our tongue, we must change our heart. It's sobering that we're accountable for every misspoken word. Often we can't wait to tell others about an offense. But the minute we talk to someone other than the person we have the issue with, we're gossiping. We rationalize that we simply need another opinion or sounding board. We may even feel justified if we're the one wronged!

However, this catharsis not only results in us sinning, but now we incriminate the person we're talking to, as she becomes a gossiping accomplice. The accomplice may be thinking, *Well, I'm only listening; I'm not going to tell anyone else.* But you can't gossip without a listening ear, so when the other person listens, you drag her into the downward sinning spiral.

My definition of gossip is repeating anything told to you in confidence, or telling another person or persons anything you know about another person that he or she didn't give you *permission* to repeat or to ask others to pray about. The person women often gossip about the most is a husband. Try saying only respectful, kind words about and to your husband and watch your marriage improve!

PERSONAL PARABLE

I wrote a skit, "Starving the Beast." The Beast is Satan, who's fed every time Christians gossip. The premise is two women gossiping about what one heard from a third party regarding the son of a mutual friend. The women decide to start a prayer chain for their friend and her son, without verifying the story or asking if their friend wants others praying. As the prayer requests spread, the story changes and escalates, eventually getting back to the furious mother.

The two women had good intentions—they didn't set out to hurt their friend. But they used prayer to perpetuate and spread gossip. Audiences tell me they were unaware of how often they feed the Beast!

Mentoring Moment

"Discretion is the better part of conversation.... God risked a lot by giving us mouths with which to praise Him and fellowship with others. We are called to be utterly trustworthy with them."
—Chris Tiegreen, *The One Year with God Devotional*, August 10.

DAY FIVE

UNMET EXPECTATIONS

onflict and disagreements often erupt from failed commitments, preconceived expectations, or betrayal from someone trusted.

ON YOUR OWN AND M&M'S

Q: What does James 1:2–5 warn about expecting everything to go the way we want in life?

Q: Read Matthew 20:1–16. What point does this story make about expectations and comparing ourselves to others?

Q: Betrayal by a friend or spouse is the ultimate unmet expectation. Someone you trusted and confided in lets you down! Perhaps this was the case with Euodia and Syntyche. Read David's anguish at the betrayal of his friend Saul (Psalm 55:12–14, 20–21). What does David conclude he should do (Psalm 55:22–23)?

Q: When someone wrongs or betrays us, what is a "natural" inclination?

- What does God say we should do instead (Leviticus 19:18 and Romans 12:17–21)?

Q: Read 1 Corinthians 6:1–8. How does Paul feel about believers suing each other?

Q: What kind of witness is it to unbelievers when Christians seek revenge?

Q: Read Luke 6:33–35. What is your reward when you lower your expectation and dismiss your felt "rights"?

Q: Read Matthew 5:38–48 and Romans 12:14. How does Jesus say we should treat those who do us wrong?

- How hard is this for you when you've been wronged? Do you think it's a fair command?

Q: How do you handle the disappointment of unmet expectations or people treating you poorly?

- If you're not pleased with your usual response, what changes are you going to make?

Q: Reread the Personal Parable in session one, day five on page 33. Have you been able to maintain a "locked door" friendship policy during unmet expectations? Explain here:

ON YOUR OWN

Q: Ask one of your Christian friends to let you know when you show signs of retaliation or seeking revenge.

M & M'S

Q: Have you had unmet expectations in your relationship, such as in setting goals? Is it possible the selected goal really wasn't what one of you wanted to do? If so, now is the time to discuss it.

Q: Be honest, in a kind way, and discuss the following questions:
- Have you met each other's expectations—as mentor or mentee?
- Is a mentoring relationship what you thought it would be?

Q: In the Woman to Woman Mentoring Ministry, the M&M'S agree to a covenant that says, "giving up on the relationship is never an option." Have you two made that kind of a "closed door" commitment to each other? If not, do that now.

FACE-TO-FACE REFLECTIONS

Most commentators agree the rift between Euodia and Syntyche probably resulted from a personality clash rather than a doctrinal issue. Likewise, the root of disagreement among Christian women usually isn't over theology, but instead: who's right, hurt feelings, misunderstandings, jealousy, broken trust, not keeping commitments, and expecting others to act and talk a certain way.

When things don't go our way or people don't treat us like we think they should, we become disappointed, frustrated, critical, angry, bitter, hurt, and maybe even resentful or want revenge—the world's way of reacting to a perceived unfair situation. Jesus asks us to do the opposite of what the world and our natural inclination tells every fiber in our body to do.

PERSONAL PARABLE

The result of unresolved conflict is two women, who were once good friends like Euodia and Syntyche, find themselves estranged and maybe even enemies. This won't happen if we commit that "no matter what," we'll stick it out and save the friendship, relationship, marriage, business, or ministry. This isn't the world's way; but throughout Jesus's teachings, He gave numerous examples to help us understand that Christians should do the exact opposite of the world's way. I call it "The Great Reversal," and here are excerpts from a poem I wrote by that name: The last shall be first. The meek will inherit the earth. The poor shall be rich. The sick will be well. The weak shall be strong. A leader is a servant. Giving is better then receiving. The exalted are humbled. The humble are exalted. Forgive our enemies. The Lion is the Lamb.

*   *   *

Mentoring Moment

"If we practice an eye for an eye and a tooth for a tooth, soon the whole world will be blind and toothless."
—Mahatma Gandhi

*   *   *

FAITH IN ACTION

What one thing from this session does God want you to apply in your life today?

LET'S PRAY TOGETHER

Lord, give us a humble heart that rejects prideful and vengeful thoughts, before we can put them into action. Help us learn how to handle anger in a healthy way so it doesn't turn into bitterness, and don't let Satan get a foothold in our hearts and minds. Lord, we want to live at peace with everyone, but it's challenging in a self-serving world. Help us keep our eyes on the bigger goal: learning ways to prevent or confront conflict and to restore broken relationships. Thank You that You always give us a second chance. Let us go and do likewise. Amen.

AGREEING
IN THE LORD

DAY ONE

WHAT'S A CHRISTIAN TO DO?

When a disagreement between Christians erupts into conflict, the Bible provides clear resolution guidelines. Paul modeled the biblical method in handling the conflict between Euodia and Syntyche.

ON YOUR OWN AND M&M'S

Q: Read Matthew 18:15–17. In what order does Jesus instruct us to deal with conflict?
   1.
   2.
   3.

- How could this biblical format prevent disagreements or misunderstandings from escalating to major conflict?

Q: How did Paul apply Matthew 18:15–17 to the conflict between Euodia and Syntyche?
   1.
   2.
   3.

- Why would Paul handle a disagreement between two people in this way?

Q: Read Galatians 2:11. How did Paul take the first step (Matthew 18:15a) in his disagreement with Peter?

Q: Explain how going directly to the offending person, or the person you offended, *"just between the two of you,"* or face-to-face, prevents the sin of gossip and slander.

• Who is to instigate the meeting (Matthew 5:23–24, 18:15)?

Q: In Philippians 4:2, Paul pleaded with Euodia and Syntyche to take the first step (Matthew 18:15a) *"to agree **with each other** in the Lord."* Using *plead* twice indicates a strong, urgent command to both of them. What is the significance of *agreeing with each other* (Matthew 18:19)?

• What do the words *"in the Lord"* add to the plea (John 17:26)?

• Note the places where Paul uses *"in the Lord"* in the Book of Philippians:

Q: Just in case Euodia and Syntyche wouldn't take the first step, Paul provided the second step (Matthew 18:15b) and asked a *"loyal yokefellow"* to intervene and help Euodia and Syntyche (Philippians 4:3). Read Galatians 3:19b–20a. What is the benefit of having a neutral mediator if you can't work things out *just between the two of you*?

• Look up the word *mediate* and write its definition here:

• Who is the mediator between God and us (1 Timothy 2:5)?

Q: Where could you find a Christian mediator if you couldn't work out a dispute?

Q: Do you follow Matthew 18:15–17 to resolve disagreements?

Face-to-Face with Euodia and Syntyche

- Why or why not?

- If not, pray for God to give you the wisdom and courage to follow His plan for dealing with disagreements.

M & M'S

Q: Commit to taking the three steps outlined in Matthew 18:15–17 to restore harmony when the two of you have an inevitable disagreement. Agree now on a mediator, should you need one later.

FACE-TO-FACE REFLECTIONS

In Philippians 4:2, Paul first begs Euodia and Syntyche to work out this dispute and get along. But sensing things had gone too far for them to agree on their own, Paul takes the second step and entreats a mediator, *"loyal yokefellow, to help these women"* (v. 3). A yoke is a wooden device to bind oxen together to work in unison. Paul asks a fellow worker (some translations say "true partner") of Paul and Euodia and Syntyche to come between the two women, put his or her arms around each woman's shoulder, and help them come together in agreement and start working in unison again.

Often when two people are quarreling, they need an independent, unbiased, and spiritually mature third party to help them see the other person's side, get perspective, and ideally, resolve the problem.

William MacDonald, in *The Believer's Bible Commentary*, describes a Christian mediator as someone who doesn't act "arbitrarily in the case and hands down a decision, but rather that by appealing to the word of God, he is able to show the contending persons the scriptural solution to their problem."

The third step of Matthew 18:15–17 was Paul's letter to the church, in which he told everyone how he, their pastor and ministry leader, felt about conflict: settle the dispute and everyone get back to work spreading the gospel of Jesus Christ.

People often take offense with policies leaders establish or enforce. You cannot please all the people all the time. A helper didn't like the way I handled a situation in the mentoring ministry, so she sent an email to my supervising pastor telling her perceptions of the event. The pastor wisely referred her to Matthew 18:15–17 and advised her first to go directly to me, and if not satisfied, to call in my assistant as a mediator. If the problem wasn't solved after taking the first two steps, then she could consult him.

She followed his advice and we were able to resolve the issue face-to-face.

Mentoring Moment

As Christians,
we should be ready to mediate when asked —
it's a biblical role.

*"I need someone to mediate between God and me,
as a person mediates between friends"* (Job 16:21 NLT).

Face-to-Face with Euodia and Syntyche

Day Two

The Power of an Apology

'm sorry. Oh, the power in those two little words and how hard it is for us to say them.

On Your Own and M&M's

Q: Why do you think Euodia and Syntyche hadn't apologized to each other already?

Q: Often we don't apologize because we feel we're right, or our pride inhibits us from admitting we're wrong. Read how God responded when He was unjustifiably wronged. What common words prevail in these situations?
- Exodus 34:6–7a
- Numbers 14:18a
- Nehemiah 9:16–19
- Psalm 103:8–11
- Jonah 4:2

Q: Read Proverbs 10:12 and 1 Corinthians 13:4–5. If God, who is *always* right, reacts in love, compassion, and forgiveness when you wrong Him, what does He want you to do when someone wrongs you?

- How hard is that for you?
- How would *acting* loving and forgiving help you offer an apology?
- What could make it easier?

Q: When you wrong someone, how often do you sincerely say, "I'm sorry for_____"? If you don't routinely apologize, why not?

- Who needs to hear those words from you right now?

Q: What words or actions might follow, "I'm sorry...," that completely negate the sincerity of the apology?

Q: Describe a time when you apologized and the person graciously received your apology.

- When you were the recipient of an apology, did you receive it graciously?

Q: Has someone been trying to apologize to you, but you won't accept the apology because:
  - ❏ You're still too angry, and you want the person to feel bad?
  - ❏ You feel no apology is sufficient?
  - ❏ You minimized the offense so you won't have to deal with that person apologizing?
  - ❏ You're embarrassed when someone apologizes?
  - ❏ List other possibilities.

Q: If apologies aren't about determining who's right or wrong, what is the purpose?

ON YOUR OWN

Q: Ask God to give you courage to offer and receive apologies.

Face-to-Face with Euodia and Syntyche

M & M'S

Q: Do either of you need to tell the other one "I'm sorry" now?

Q: Confess if there's anyone you owe an apology. Help each other follow through.

Q: Discuss the dynamics of letting someone apologize to you. Pray together to be a gracious recipient and extender of apologies.

FACE-TO-FACE REFLECTIONS

I was surprised to see this online news: "Oprah apologizes for slamming author James Frey." Frey had appeared on Winfrey's program to apologize publicly for lying to her about his memoir; but feeling betrayed, Oprah berated Frey but later apologized.

Apologies should be specific and take ownership for the offense, as Frey did. That doesn't always assure the acceptance of your apology, but it's still the right thing to do. Accepting an apology doesn't condone the offense. Oprah's apology didn't condone Frey's lying, but conveyed: *I'm sorry for not receiving your apology.*

As hard as it is to apologize, some of us aren't good at receiving apologies. We minimize the offense by shrugging off the apology: that's dishonest. Or we refuse to let the person off the hook: that's vengeful.

In the article, *The Power of an Apology,* Rosamund Stone Zander wrote advice to help restore harmony:

When you blame someone, you get resistance. But if you take responsibility for repairing a rift, you form a team....

Once you realize you don't have to make yourself wrong to deliver an apology, you'll feel a new power.

1. Think of any breakdown between you and another person as an opportunity to apologize. You know there is a breakdown when you feel angry, tense, disapproving, distant, sad, or vengeful toward someone.

2. Notice that the way you are feeling and behaving is maintaining the problem.

3. Apologize for letting anything other than the relationship take priority: For example, say: "I'm sorry that I let my feelings of pride (or fear or laziness) get in the way of us."

Only a sincere, heartfelt apology appeases. While talking on the phone to my daughter Kim, I overheard three-year-old, Katelyn, hit her four-year-old brother, Brandon. Kim scolded Katelyn and told her to tell Brandon she was sorry. Katelyn gave a lighthearted "Sorry," to which Brandon cried, "It doesn't matter!" I told Kim that Brandon knew Katelyn's apology wasn't sincere. She only said it to get out of trouble, and Brandon wasn't buying it.

Sometimes, I'm just like my granddaughter. My husband and I were driving to church with an unresolved conflict lingering between us. Knowing we couldn't worship without resolving our issue, I courageously apologized. However as "I'm sorry" exited my mouth, I quickly interjected, "But I still think...."

My husband retorted, "I'm trying to figure out why your apology is making me so angry?"

Adding *but* negated my apology. I communicated: I'll do the Christian thing and apologize. *But* I'm still right! I was getting in the last word. Isn't that often what keeps us from taking the first step to apologize? We feel if we're right, they should apologize or at least acknowledge they were wrong.

The real purpose of an apology, however, is to knit the relationship back together again, regardless of who's right or wrong. When you get it right, "I'm sorry," is redemption!

Mentoring Moment

"The power of an apology does not lie in the admission of guilt. An apology is a tool to affirm the primacy of our connection with others. It can unlock deep love in our everyday lives. Don't wait. Apologize!"—Chinese philosopher Lao-Tse more than 2,000 years ago, *The Power of an Apology*

Face-to-Face with Euodia and Syntyche

Day Three

Choose Your Mountains

renda Hunter tells a story of a Southern Baptist minister friend of hers who once overheard some parishioners decimate his preaching style as they stood outside his office, not realizing he was inside. Brenda writes: "He elected not to confront them because he says, 'Choose the mountains you die on.'" Choosing not to confront an issue doesn't mean stuffing it. If you can't let it go, then bring it up.

On Your Own and M&M's

Q: Proverbs 17:14 (TLB) warns, *"It is hard to stop a quarrel once it starts, so don't let it begin."* How does Proverbs 17:14 read in your Bible?

Q: How does Paul say to discern which conflict mountains to climb (Philippians 1:9–10)?

Q: In Philippians 1:15–18, what was Paul's position regarding those who were trying to stir up trouble for him?

Q: What did Paul advise the church at Philippi to do in order to keep disagreements in perspective and prevent future quarrels (Philippians 3:15–4:1)?

- Explain how verses 3:15–21 establish Paul's case for admonishing Euodia and Syntyche in 4:2–3, and verse 4:1 segues between the two areas of discussion.

Q: When Nehemiah was rebuilding the wall of Jerusalem, he had angry opponents trying to discourage him (Nehemiah 4:1–12).
- How did Nehemiah decide to handle the conflict (6:1–4)?

- When opposition persisted, how did he reply (vv. 8–9)?
- What did he do next (v. 9)?

Q: Read Ecclesiastes 3:8. Explain how this verse, Nehemiah's actions, and the advice from Paul to the Philippians can help you determine when to confront and when to let the issue go:

Q: Describe an occasion where you quietly chose to forgive without confronting the issue:

- Were you able to move on, or did you continue to let the issue fester?
- How did your decision make you feel?

M & M'S

Q: Mentor, discuss with your mentee the difference between quietly forgiving without confronting, versus avoiding an issue.

FACE-TO-FACE REFLECTIONS

It's possible you couldn't remember a time you quietly chose to forgive, because if you truly were able to let it go, you might not remember it now. We'll talk more about forgiveness in the next session.

However, if the memory of "letting something go" brought back any ill feelings, or you treat that person any differently than before the incident, you haven't forgiven completely and will want to take the "7 Biblical Steps to Resolving Conflict" in this session, day five.

Sometimes, it helps to step back and consider: Is this issue that important? As Paul concluded in Philippians 1:18, *"But what does it matter?"*

Mentoring Moment

"I do not intend to get...into endless arguments and discussion with them [the press].... I am going to take the position of Nehemiah when he refused to go down and have a conference with his enemies. He said, 'I'm too busy building the wall.' We are too busy winning souls to Christ and helping build the church to go down and argue."
—Billy Graham, *Ruth: A Portrait: The Story of Ruth Bell Graham*

session three

Day Four

Agreeing to Disagree

We've acknowledged that even as Christian women, we're going to disagree. Harmony may mean agreeing to disagree.

On Your Own and M&M's

Q: Read Acts 15:36–41 and note how Paul handled a disagreement with his fellow missionary and mentor, Barnabas:

Q: Now read how Paul later refers to Barnabas and Mark (1 Corinthians 9:6 and 2 Timothy 4:11):

Q: Paul wrote the letter to the Philippians about 11 years after the disagreement with Barnabas. What do you think Paul learned regarding how to agree to disagree and reconcile with fellow workers for Christ, as he matured in his faith?

Q: In Philippians 3:17 and 4:9 Paul tells the church to follow his example. Who helped Paul change his ways (Philippians 3:7–12 and 1 Corinthians 11:1)?

Q: Look back at the first question in session one, day one, where you described a relationship that ended because you had a disagreement. Based on your spiritual maturity and what you're learning in this study, what could you have done differently to restore and save that relationship?

- It's not too late. Maybe God is asking you to build a bridge back to that person by apologizing and then taking steps to reconcile, even if you both still have a different point of view. Keep that in mind as you continue working through this study.

M & M'S

Q: You committed to this M&M relationship so giving up is not an option, even when you disagree—especially when you disagree! Take a moment at your next meeting to reconfirm your commitment to each other.

Q: If there's someone from either of your pasts who you need to agree to disagree with, then pray and encourage each other to contact that person. Mentor, like Paul, set an example for your mentee to follow regarding how to resolve conflict and live a mature life in Christ.

FACE-TO-FACE REFLECTIONS

Paul specifically says that Euodia and Syntyche must not only stop fighting, but they must *agree in the Lord*. Maybe they will agree to disagree, but the friendship continues, and most importantly, the ministry work resumes. We shouldn't throw in the towel on a relationship the first time there's conflict—just like we don't get a divorce every time we disagree with our husband. Sadly, today many people do exactly that. They give up when the going gets a little tough, but that's not the Lord's way, unless there's imminent danger or harm.

Most often, we're to swallow our pride, take the first step toward resolving the problem, say, "I'm sorry," and acknowledge the other person's right to disagree for the betterment of the relationship and the Lord's work.

When M&M'S disagree on issues, they sometimes think they aren't a good match. Actually that might be exactly why God wanted them together. He often puts us in the very situations where He knows we need the most work.

PERSONAL PARABLE

In the Woman to Woman Mentoring Ministry, we match M&M'S through intercessory prayer. Maybe God will put together a stay-at-home mom with a working mom. At first, it might seem they have nothing in common, as they disagree over whether a mother should stay home or work.

We help the M&M'S consider that maybe God wants them to develop understanding and compassion for the other's situation without judging or condemning.

Jane, a stay-at-home mom at the time, mentored a working woman with no kids. The two women thought they had nothing in common, but soon discovered that God wanted them to learn from each other. Jane and her husband led a small group, and her mentee wanted tips for including her husband in leadership of their group. Both women had very similar styles of humor and communication. Initially thinking they might disagree, they discovered they did agree on a spiritual friendship and serving the Lord.

Mentoring Moment

You don't need to see eye-to-eye to connect heart-to-heart.

DAY FIVE

7 BIBLICAL STEPS TO RESOLVING CONFLICT

*T*he followng tool will help you apply what you've learned in this session. These "7 Biblical Steps to Resolving Conflict," are adapted from Brenda Hunter's *In the Company of Women*, included in my book *Praying for Your Prodigal Daughter*. Each step is based on Scripture, many of which we have studied.

ON YOUR OWN AND M&M'S

Q: Read each step and look up the supporting Scriptures. Pray together before going through these steps.

1. *Take the initiative to resolve the conflict* (Matthew 5:23–24, 18:15–17). The moment you sense a problem in your relationship, take the first step toward righting it—even if you think the other person was wrong and you've done nothing to provoke her. If possible, approach her face-to-face. Letters, e-mail, texting, or phone calls seldom resolve conflict because we can't read each other's face, eyes, or body language.

   If face-to-face is not feasible, use the phone so you can proceed with the following steps. But the phone is *only* an option when it's the only option.

   If she won't meet alone, offer to bring a nonbiased mediator. If that's disagreeable, meet with a pastor from church.

2. *Focus on goals bigger than your personal differences* (Ephesians 4:3; Philippians 3:12–14). Before starting a discussion, establish that the relationship is more important than any disagreement.

3. *Listen attentively as the other person tells how she sees the situation* (Proverbs 18:13; Proverbs 29:20).Let her speak first while you *listen* with your heart, eyes, and ears without becoming defensive or angry. Empathize as you hear the hurt in her voice. Don't interrupt. Let her complete her story.

4. *Validate the other person's feelings without minimizing her concerns* (James 1:19–20). Acknowledge her points, without arguing or challenging. Then ask if she'll listen to you.

5. *Tell your story* (Proverbs 18:17). Indicate you understand how she may have *perceived* the situation differently than you meant it. Avoid assigning blame. It's OK to let her know how the situation hurt your feelings.

6. *Apologize and ask forgiveness for your part in the disagreement* (Colossians 3:13 and 1 John 1:9–10). Don't expect her to say she's sorry or to ask for forgiveness. Forgive with no hidden agenda or expectations. Session four provides a more in-depth discussion of forgiveness.

7. *Discuss how to avoid future conflict* (Proverbs 17:14). Set ground rules for the relationship. Close with prayer.

ON YOUR OWN

Q: Ask a friend to help you practice going through these steps. When ready, use the steps in conflict situations.

M&M'S

Q: Discuss each of the "7 Biblical Steps to Resolving Conflict," then practice working through a fictitious or real conflict. Discuss any questions about a step.

FACE-TO-FACE REFLECTIONS

When I speak on these steps, women tell me it's the first time they've heard how to resolve conflict peacefully and biblically.

An important caveat is applying these steps when the Holy Spirit convicts you that someone has a grudge against you, or you have one against someone else. Don't procrastinate. Make the phone call, and set an appointment to get together. Meet in a neutral spot like a coffee house, restaurant, or park. Take two copies of the "7 Biblical Steps to Resolving Conflict," and if you feel comfortable, give one to the other person. Then you both can stay on track. You'll be amazed how quickly problems are resolved.

From personal experience, the most difficult step after making the initial contact will be sitting quietly while you let the other person tell her version of the story. Let me warn, if you interrupt or try setting the record straight before she has finished talking, you'll escalate the argument and accomplish nothing. Listening to both sides of the story often reveals that the issue was only a misunderstanding or misperception of words or actions.

Another difficult step will be apologizing—especially if you don't think you're in the wrong. Try being sorry she has hurt feelings; even if you don't think they're justified, she's hurting. And it can't be an apology with a hook: you expect her to apologize in return. She may not, but your apology should still be sincere. We'll talk more next session about why we forgive and how to forgive.

· ·

PERSONAL PARABLE

Marty Norman, in her book *Generation G*, tells the story of resolving a marital conflict by altering her perspective on the problem. Steps 3–5 in "7 Biblical Steps to Resolving Conflict," always present a fresh perspective, for both sides.

I was sitting on a bench, trying to reconcile conflict in my marriage. In front of me was a large tree. Interspersed with its green, perfectly shaped branches were long bare branches resembling scarecrow arms. I couldn't imagine what kind of tree this was. Not until I moved to a different spot on the bench did I realize I was actually looking at two trees, one directly in front of the other. At that moment, I was presented with truth. Position affects perception; perception affects perspective. I was able to look at my own situation in a new light. My conflict became clearer because I had changed my position. Looking at the conflict from another perspective, I was astounded by what I saw.

*   *   *

Mentoring Moment

"Learning how to resolve conflict the biblical way allows us to keep our cool and humbly communicate in a peaceful, loving manner—Christ's way. Unresolved conflict can cause unrest, disunity, anger, revenge, yelling, and screaming—Satan's way. When we resist Satan by adopting Christlike behavior, the enemy retreats—at least for the moment. He'll be back with a new strategy, but don't allow him to get a foothold."—Janet Thompson, *Praying for Your Prodigal Daughter*

*   *   *

FAITH IN ACTION

Q: What one thing from this session does God want you to apply in your life today?

LET'S PRAY TOGETHER

Lord, You gave us tools to resolve conflict; we just need to apply them. Please convict and give us courage to be the initiator in resolving conflicts Your way, not the world's way. Put in us a quiet and gentle spirit that doesn't make an issue out of every disagreement, and help us remember not everyone has to agree with us to be our friend. Lord, You, who are holy and righteous, had people spit on You, and You didn't retaliate. You're our role model of humble strength. We love You, Lord. Amen.

FOREVER
FORGIVEN

DAY ONE

WE FORGIVE
BECAUSE WE WERE FORGIVEN

One moment Euodia and Syntyche were effectively working side-by-side with their fellow evangelists. The next, they were arguing and work came to an abrupt halt. The only way to continue serving the Lord with a clean heart was to settle the problem and eliminate unforgiveness. Otherwise, the issues would fester and erupt again. Perhaps the women needed a reminder of how Christ forgave them.

ON YOUR OWN AND M&M'S

Q: Read Micah 7:18–19. How forgiving is God?

Q: What are the conditions for receiving God's unconditional forgiveness?
- Matthew 6:12, 14–15
- Mark 2:5
- Mark 11:25–26
- Luke 6:37
- Acts 10:43
- 1 John 1:9

Q: Who has authority to forgive our sins (Matthew 9:2–7 and Ephesians 1:3, 7)?

Q: What does John 20:21–23 say our role should be in helping people receive God's forgiveness?

Q: Read Mark 3:28–29. What is one sin God won't forgive, and why is it unforgivable?

Q: How do we receive salvation (Luke 1:76–79; John 3:14–18)?

Q: Read Luke 7:47. What is evidence that God forgave us?

Q: Who is our role model of forgiving the seemingly unforgivable (Luke 23:33–34)?
- Why did Jesus say those who crucified Him didn't know what they were doing?

Q: How does remembering God's unconditional forgiveness help you keep in perspective what your response should be when others hurt you (Colossians 3:13)?

Q: How does undeserved forgiveness witness to unbelievers?

ON YOUR OWN

Q: If you have questions about the Scriptures regarding God's forgiveness and our forgiving others, find someone who can mentor you through this process.

Q: To receive God's forgiveness for your sins, pray the Salvation Prayer on page 32, confessing your sins, and knowing Jesus is faithful to forgive *all* your sins. Then you'll be able to forgive those who hurt you.

M & M'S

Q: Mentor, ask your mentee if she has questions regarding today's Scriptures and interpretation.

Q: Mentee, if you haven't accepted Christ's forgiveness, talk with your mentor about concerns. When ready, go to the Salvation Prayer on page 32, God will forgive your sins and you'll be equipped to forgive others.

In *The Soul Bible*, Everett L. Worthington Jr. provides a descriptive word picture of forgiveness, "The concept of forgiveness is as slippery as a greased watermelon in a swimming pool. The harder you squeeze it, the more slippery it becomes."

Forgiveness forgets the words *fair*, *right*, and *just compensation* — words we often use to justify not forgiving others. God doesn't consider these words when He looks at us.

Forgiveness is an act of the will, not of emotion. We forgive because *we are* forgiven. We must replace emotions of hurt or betrayal with God's truths. Replace anger with mercy and grace — resentment with restoration — bitterness with brotherly/sisterly love. Pray sincerely for the betterment of your offenders — maybe they need the Lord in their life, or they have an addiction or loss. The Holy Spirit will direct your prayers.

God doesn't forgive others because we forgive them, nor does He withhold forgiveness because we choose not to forgive. But we can be instrumental in someone receiving God's forgiveness by sparking her curiosity about how we can be so forgiving; or our *unforgiveness* could do the complete opposite.

Forgiveness is possible through the power of the indwelling Holy Spirit when we accept the grace and forgiveness of Jesus Christ into our hearts and souls. Then we're capable of extending that same forgiveness to others. If God forgives undeserving sinners like us, how can we do any less to those who wrong us?

In her book *Tramp for the Lord*, Corrie ten Boom tells the story of her sister Betsie dying in Ravensbrück camp, where both endured imprisonment in 1944 for helping Jews. Years later, one of the cruelest camp guards approached Corrie, who was reluctant to forgive him, but prayed she could: "For a long moment we grasped each other's hands, the former guard, and the former prisoner. I had never known God's love so intensely as I did then."

Corrie also wrote that in her post-war experience with other victims of Nazi brutality, those who were able to forgive were best able to rebuild their lives.

In his book, *Murder By Family: The Incredible True Story of a Son's Treachery and a Father's Forgiveness*, Keith Whitaker recalls the shooting of his family. Keith's wife and younger son died, but Keith and his oldest son, Bart, survived. Keith, a longtime Christian, chose to forgive the seemingly unforgivable, because God had forgiven him.

So here I was, in the middle of a horrific situation in which I had to choose to either go with my feelings and slip into bitterness and despair, or follow my own advice and stand on God's promises even when they don't make sense.

When I resolved to trust God, I felt a peace come over me....Then the next thought popped unexpectedly into my mind: What about the shooter?

I realized that God was offering me the ability to forgive, if I wanted to take advantage of it.... I know the Bible says we are to forgive those who hurt us. I know God tells us that vengeance is his, if he chooses to dispense it.... But did I really want to forgive, even if God was offering a supernatural ability to do so.

In an instant the answer sprang full-grown into my mind. My heart told me that I wanted whoever was responsible to come to Christ and repent for this awful act. At that moment I felt myself completely forgiving him.... Little did I realize just how important my decision to forgive would be in the coming months. It would change everything.

Mentoring Moment

"I put Jesus on the Cross and God forgave me."
—Pastor Tim Westcott

Day Two

Mercy and Grace

Fred Luskin, a Stanford University researcher, gave a talk at a church in my area, and he quoted novelist Frederick Buechner, who characterized the affects of an unforgiving heart: "To lick your wounds, to smack your lips over grievances long past, to roll over your tongue the prospect of bitter confrontations still to come, to savor to the last toothsome morsel both the pain you are given and the pain you are giving back—in many ways it is a feast fit for a King. The chief drawback is that you are wolfing down yourself."

On Your Own and M&M's

Q: How do we receive God's mercy (Proverbs 28:13 and Romans 9:15–16)?

Q: What is the *"gospel of God's grace"* (Acts 20:24)?
- Romans 5:1–2, 8, 19–21
- Ephesians 1:3–8
- Ephesians 4:7

Q: What does Scripture warn about having a resentful, revengeful, unforgiving heart?
- Job 5:2
- Proverbs 20:22
- Zechariah 7:10*b*

Q: Read Hebrew 12:14–15. *Bitterroot* could include pride, animosity, rivalry, or anything harmful to others.

- How could not forgiving someone possibly cause her to miss God's grace?

- How could being unforgiving cause a bitter root to grow in your heart?

Q: Read Ephesians 2:1–10 then answer these questions:
- Before we were Christians, what were all of us (vv. 1–3)?

- How are we saved (vv. 5, 8)?

- Who gives the gift of salvation (v. 8)?

- What is God rich in toward us (vv. 4, 7)?

Q: Read John 1:14. What does it mean to be full of grace *and* truth?

- Who is the only perfect manifestation of grace *and* truth?

- Why's it hard to find a balance between excusing and legalism?

Q: What do these verses teach about God wanting us to extend mercy and grace?
- Micah 6:8
- Zechariah 7:8–9
- Matthew 5:7
- James 2:12–13

Q: God showed mercy and grace to us—sinners who deserved judgment—what does He want us to do in return (Luke 6:36)?

Q: God will make all things right in His time and in His way. Where does justice originate (Proverbs 29:26)?

- Are you confident enough in God's sovereignty to let Him determine justice? Why or why not?

Q: Write your own definition of:
- Truth
- Justice
- Mercy
- Grace

Q: What does the opening quote by Frederick Buechner mean to you personally?

Q: Describe a time you didn't show mercy or grace and remained judgmental and unforgiving. How did it feel?

- Were you ever able to forgive? Why or why not?

Q: When have you extended grace to someone who offended you, instead of seeking justice and how did that feel?

M & M'S

Q: Talk about ways to be both gracious and truthful with each other. Make notes here:

FACE-TO-FACE REFLECTIONS

Mercy is showing more love and kindness to a person than she expects or deserves. Grace is undeserved forgiveness. Truth without grace is legalistic and crushes; grace without truth is deceptive and cowardly. A balance of lovingly and truthfully extending grace to others restores relationships and sets us free from replayed anger, hurt, bitterness, hatred, hostility, or fear.

I heard a woman interviewed on television after her release from prison for killing her father, who allegedly abused her since childhood. While in prison, she forgave her father: "I had to forgive him for his actions so I could forgive myself for mine. Unforgiveness is a prison." After forgiving him she said, "I was free. I was still in prison, but that was just geography."

Satan doesn't want us to experience the freedom of extending mercy and grace to those who hurt us, or forgiving ourselves.

Imagine your heart and emotions held captive by Satan as he manipulates your thoughts and actions! Startling thought, isn't it? But that's exactly what transpires in your soul when you don't forgive.

The keys to emotional freedom are mercy, grace, and forgiveness. The same keys Christ used to set your soul free of Satan's grip. Then you're ready to love others and serve Christ. Hallelujah!

PERSONAL PARABLE

Kent Whitaker's story from *Murder by Family* continued:
I have had a hundred people tell me that they think I'm nuts—that I should hate the shooter and cry out for vengeance. Perhaps I am crazy, but I believe that in those early moments God worked supernaturally, allowing me to forgive completely and immediately because he had plans for me, and those plans required that I settle the forgiveness problem once and for all.

The killer Keith mercifully and graciously chose to forgive, instead of demanding justice, turned out to be his own son, Bart! However, the courts chose justice and Bart is on death row.

Mentoring Moment

Justice is getting what you deserve.
Mercy is *not* getting everything you deserve.
Grace is getting what you don't deserve.
—Pastor Tim Westcott

DAY THREE

MYTHS AND TRUTHS

Many people never forgive because they think extending forgiveness means condoning behavior or conceding. Others think forgiving requires reconciling even if a person hasn't changed or still is harmful. Let's investigate some of the forgiveness myths and replace them with truths.

ON YOUR OWN AND M&M'S

Q: Look up these words in a dictionary and write the definitions:
● *Forgive*

● *Reconcile*

Q: What is the main difference between the two?

Q: How many people does it take to forgive?

Q: How many people does it take to reconcile?

Q: Match the *myth* with the *truth* by drawing a line between the two.

Forgiveness Myth	Forgiveness Truth
1. Must be quick like God's forgiveness	A. Doesn't make sin OK
	B. Is a process
2. Condones the offense	C. Doesn't require reconciliation
3. Requires forgetting, like God does	
	D. Doesn't require forgetting
4. Necessitates reconciliation	E. Other person doesn't have to apologize
5. Doesn't require personal involvement	
	F. Offender may never change
6. Offender has to make atonement	G. Not OK for offender to repeat offense
7. Obligates offender to ask for forgiveness	H. Can only forgive offense against you
8. Let's offender off the hook	I. Offender doesn't have to ask forgiveness
9. Frees offender to do it again	
10. Means offender has to change	J. Offender still has consequences

Q: Which myths have you believed?

Q: Read John 8:31–32. How has learning the truths about forgiveness set you free to forgive?

M & M'S

Q: Discuss how you did with matching the myths and truths. If either of you believed a myth, share how learning the truth will change how you approach forgiveness.

FACE-TO-FACE REFLECTIONS

Here are the answers for the "Forgiveness Myth or Truth" matching.
1. B—The Bible, from Genesis 3 to the Cross, records God's process of forgiving His people. Jesus's words on the Cross,

"It is finished," signified that God's forgiving process was over. Now He forgives quickly, but in our humanness, we may need time. You can choose to forgive immediately, but work through your feelings.

2. A — Forgiveness doesn't condone the offense: it's choosing to forgive *in spite* of what the offender did.

3. D — You may need to remember the circumstances so you aren't hurt again. We learn from our mistakes, bad choices, reactions, and experiences: they're a reminder to avoid certain types of people, temptations, situations, and to make better choices and responses in the future.

4. C — Forgiveness is unilateral: *I* do it. It's vertical between you and the Lord. Reconciliation is bilateral: *we* do it. It's horizontal between two forgiving people, but not with a harmful person.

5. H — Only the offended can forgive the offender.

6. E — You cannot forgive with a hook: manipulating or expecting compensation for the offense.

7. I — Forgiveness freely given doesn't rely on the other person receiving your forgiveness or forgiving you. Forgive in your heart and move on to your own healing and improved life.

8. J — The offender is responsible for whatever damage that person did or consequences to their actions.

9. G — Forgiving doesn't victimize you. Avoid an offender who hasn't changed.

10. F — The offender may never change, but forgiveness will change you.

PERSONAL PARABLE

I labored under forgiveness myths during a 15-year estrangement from my mother. One day in church, Pastor Rick Warren gave a sermon on forgiveness. He said you'll never experience true love if you have a bitter unforgiving heart. I was single and realized if I didn't forgive my mother, I could never love a husband.

Pastor Rick said it didn't matter if the person was dead or alive, or whether they deserved forgiveness or not. He

Face-to-Face with Euodia and Syntyche

said many of us let dead people continue to hurt us. How ridiculous is that! Since forgiveness is between you and God, you can forgive that person—right now!

Over the years, I had approached my mother about "burying the hatchet," but she suffered under the myth that forgiveness meant reliving each incident and assigning blame. In session two, I told the story of watching anger and bitterness eat away at my mother over the death of my father, and eventually, I became the recipient of her unforgiving heart.

I couldn't do anything about her feelings about my father's death, but I could change the dynamics between my mother and me. I understood the truth that I didn't have to wait until we both felt the same way; it only took one of us to forgive.

After much prayer, I visited my mom and told her I forgave her and asked for her forgiveness. Even though she was resistant—didn't forgive me, didn't receive my forgiveness, or ask me for forgiveness—I still forgave her. My unforgiving heart was set free!

My mother died several months later and in her last Will and Testament, she disinherited my sister and me. My mom hadn't changed, but *I* had changed, and nothing she did could hurt me again. What freedom! Freedom that allowed me to meet the man God had planned for me to marry and go into that relationship with a heart ready to freely give and receive love.

Mentoring Moment

"Don't fall into the trap of thinking you're doing the person a favor by forgiving him. The favor is for you."
—Bob Enright, *Forgiveness Is a Choice*

"To worry yourself to death with resentment would be a foolish, senseless thing to do" (Job 5:2 GNT).

DAY FOUR

KNOWING HOW TO FORGIVE

*W*hy is it so hard to forgive? As Christians, we know we should forgive, but it can never be a *duty* of the mind and will: it must be an *action* of the heart. Forgiveness is a choice — our choice.

ON YOUR OWN AND M&M'S

Q: What do you learn from the following verses about how to forgive like God forgives?
- Jeremiah 31:33–34
- Jeremiah 33:8
- John 8:1–11
- Ephesians 4:2, 22–27

Q: What is the Lord full of that He can so easily forgive us (Psalm 103:2–4,8,13)?

Q: How will showing love, mercy, and compassion help you take forgiving steps?
- Psalm 119:77–78
- Ephesians 4:30–5:1

Q: Read 2 Corinthians 2:5–11 and Galatians 6:1–3. How are we to forgive and restore a fellow Christian who falters spiritually, accepts discipline, repents, and asks for forgiveness?

Q: What prevents you forgiving someone who offends you?

Q: How readily do you ask others for forgiveness?

ON YOUR OWN

Q: If you know *why* you should forgive, but still have trouble knowing *how* to forgive, the "Five Steps to Forgiveness" in the Face-to-Face Reflections should help you. For some of the steps, it's advisable to have someone go through them with you. This would be a perfect time to find a mentor.

M & M'S

Q: Sometime in your M&M relationship, one of you is going to have to forgive the other. Make a commitment that you'll practice the "Five Steps to Forgiveness" in Face-to-Face Reflections.

Q: If you've identified someone you need to forgive, help each other take the five steps.

FACE-TO-FACE REFLECTIONS

Psychologist Everett L. Worthington, Jr., author of *Five Steps to Forgiveness*, wrote an essay in *The Soul Bible* putting these five steps into an acrostic: R E A C H. As you consider each step, which I have paraphrased and enhanced, consider that Worthington published his book several years after a teenage robber killed his mother in her home.

1. *Recall* the hurt objectively: focus on facts, not victimization. Don't deny, but don't dwell on the offense. This can be painful and intense: have someone grieve with you.

2. *Empathize* with the offender. Put yourself in their shoes and visualize what might have motivated them. If that's too difficult, try replacing anger with compassion or sympathy.

3. Give an *Altruistic* gift of forgiveness. Worthington suggests we recall when we harmed someone who later forgave us. Remember what happened and how you received the offer of forgiveness. Then you can more easily see yourself giving that gift back to another.

4. **Commit** publicly your forgiving act by telling a trusted friend, journaling, or maybe sending a letter to the offender. The public commitment solidifies your forgiveness.

5. **Hold onto** forgiveness. You may not forget the offense; but *do* recall the forgiveness. There's a difference between *remembering* the event and *experiencing* the emotions or doubting your forgiveness. If you replay the event, replay the forgiveness.

PERSONAL PARABLE

The REACH steps work! When I forgave my mom, I didn't realize I was using these five steps, but I now see my actions modeled them.

Recall — I remembered my mom's offenses, while keeping in perspective the mistakes I'd made.

Empathize — I considered how hard it was for her to be a widow raising two girls, without having the Lord in her life.

Altruistic gift — I decided to forgive her and gave her the gift of forgiveness she didn't request or reciprocate.

Commit publicly — I went public by taking my teenage daughter, Kim, and my sister with me. I've written and spoken many times about forgiving my mother.

Hold onto forgiveness — Even Mom disowning me didn't affect my forgiveness. I've experienced the real freedom that comes from the kind of forgiveness only the Lord offers, and I pray you experience it too.

Mentoring Moment

"If we are going to take God's principles seriously, we will see that forgiveness isn't optional. It is essential. What is optional is whether we choose the quick and easy path of superficial forgiveness, or the harder but more rewarding path of genuine forgiveness." Dr. David Stoop and Dr. James Mateller, *Forgiving Our Parents Forgiving Ourselves*

Face-to-Face with Euodia and Syntyche

DAY FIVE

UNCONDITIONAL FORGIVENESS

*F*orgiving unconditionally means never taking it back! We may have to forgive the same person repeatedly for new offenses, but each incident is a new act of forgiveness. Even if the other person denies, excuses, or becomes offended, that doesn't influence our decision to forgive.

ON YOUR OWN AND M&M'S

Q: Read the story of the unforgiving servant in Matthew 18:23–35. How sincere must our forgiveness be?

Q: Some two decades after Joseph's brothers betrayed and sold him into slavery—time enough for Joseph to harbor resentment and vengeance—God reunited Joseph with his jealous brothers. Yet, what did Joseph say to his brothers in Genesis 45:4–11?

- How hard was this for his brothers to believe (Genesis 50:15–18)?
- What was Joseph's response of unconditional forgiveness (Genesis 50:19–21)?

Q: It's not easy forgiving unconditionally—not carrying a grudge or a desire to get even. Read Romans 12:14–21. Who will rectify the situation, if needed (v.19)?

Q: How often are we to forgive others (Matthew 18:21–22 and Luke 17:3–4)?

Q: Read Hebrews 8:12. Just as Jesus does with us, what are we supposed to do after we forgive?

• Do you feel God unconditionally forgave and forgot your sins? Explain.

• How difficult is it to forgive someone and never bring up the subject again, even in your mind?

• If you've unconditionally forgiven someone, describe how that feels.

Q: What specific concepts from session four will help you with forgiveness in the future?

ON YOUR OWN

Q: If you've "forgiven" someone, but the offense still haunts you, what would help you *unconditionally* forgive now?

• Tell someone when you extend this gift of unconditional forgiveness.

M & M'S

Q: You've each probably forgiven someone then brought the offense back up in your mind or to the offender. Unconditionally forgive that person in front of each other right now.

• If the person you unconditionally forgave is living, keep each other accountable to contacting him/her and extending the gift of unconditional forgiveness—even if you already "forgave" or they don't know they offended you.

FACE-TO-FACE REFLECTIONS

Not feeling unconditionally forgiven or worthy of forgiveness impairs the ability to unconditionally forgive. Unresolved guilt or anger manifests itself in judgmental or critical behavior that keeps someone trapped in a cycle of insecurity and resentment.

There's a movie about a recovering drug addict, whose past drug-related accident resulted in the death of her younger brother. At an AA meeting, she admitted,

> I struggle with God so much because I can't forgive myself, and I don't really want to right now. I can live with it, but I can't forgive myself. And sometimes I don't want to believe in a God that could forgive me.
>
> If I hurt someone...I hurt someone. I can apologize and they can forgive me or not. But I can change. I just wanted to share that. And say congratulations that God makes you look up and I'm so happy for you; but if He doesn't, come here (AA meeting).

Like the movie character, you may feel God couldn't forgive you for your past, and if He did, what kind of a God is He? The answer: He's a gracious God who sent His Son, Jesus, to die for your sins that were unforgivable any other way. The young woman in the movie was right: if you are still haunted by your or another's past sins, you do need to seek out a believer who can help you experience God's forgiveness. It's important for you to find a mentor, or talk to a pastor, because I want you to experience the freedom of unconditional forgiveness.

Unconditional forgiveness of others and yourself doesn't happen at will. It takes time and prayer; but it's an essential step to healing relationships and yourself. An accountability partner can help identify areas where you haven't forgiven or don't feel forgiven.

Unconditional forgiveness means giving up the right to visit an incident ever again. When asked how many times we should forgive, *"Jesus answered, 'I tell you, not seven times, but seventy-seven times'"* (Matthew 18:22). If you're counting, it doesn't count.

In the chapter, Extending Unconditional Forgiveness in my book, *Praying for Your Prodigal Daughter,* I recount my daughter Kim's first awareness of her softened heart and renewed mind that Christ granted her after she committed her life to Him. Her first step as a new Christian was extending unconditional forgiveness.

Mom, when you and Dad first divorced, I saw my dad frequently. Over the years, I saw less and less of him. I missed him and the relationship we once had, and I know I've made many wrong choices trying to fill that void in my life. I became angry and resentful of the consequences of the divorce. I plotted how one day I would get revenge. That was until Toby [her fiancé] and I both accepted Christ, and I felt my heart starting to change.

I remember telling you through tears and sobs about my new, strange feelings of suddenly not wanting revenge but wanting to forgive instead. I asked you, 'Is this what it means to be a Christian—to forgive those who had hurt me?' You said yes.

I find forgiveness is a daily process. However, I know what it feels like to operate out of revenge and anger, and I never want to go back to letting bitterness control my feelings.

• • •

Mentoring Moment

"Those of us who have worked through the process of forgiveness have the deep satisfaction of knowing that we can survive injury — and not only survive, but flourish. No matter how deep the wound, no matter how bitter the pain, once we forgive, we are no longer victims or mere survivors. We are victors! We have fought through to the ultimate triumph. We have learned to love."
— Dr. David Stoop and Dr. James Masteller,
Forgiving Our Parents Forgiving Ourselves

• • •

FAITH IN ACTION

What one thing from this session does God want you to apply in your life today?

LET'S PRAY TOGETHER

Dear Father, thank You for Your unconditional love and forgiveness. Sometimes it's hard to forgive others as You forgave us. Lord, we need help applying Your Word to our life. Our flesh and pride holds us back from receiving the redeeming freedom that comes with letting go of the unforgiveness that holds us captive. We want to move on. Lord, grant us peace and tranquility that comes from releasing our pain into Your welcoming arms. We know we can do all things through You! Amen.

FROM CONFLICT
TO COMMUNITY

Day One

The Ministry of Reconciliation

*I*n *Experiencing God Day-by-Day*, Henry T. and Richard Blackaby challenge believers: "As Christians, we are appointed as ministers of reconciliation. Once Christ dwells within us, we become his ambassadors, and we entreat others to be reconciled to him (2 Corinthians 5:20). We urge reconciliation first with God, and then with each other."

On Your Own and M&M's

Q: Read Ephesians 6:19–20. What does it mean to be an "ambassador for Christ"?

Q: Read 2 Corinthians 5:18–21. What do these verses tell you about the "ministry of reconciliation"?
- Who first reconciled with us (v. 18)?
- What ministry did God then give to us (v. 18)?
- What has Christ committed to us (v. 19)?
- What is our job for Christ (v. 20)?

Q: God doesn't want our gifts if we aren't reconciled with other believers (Matthew 5:23–24). What gifts would God not want from Euodia and Syntyche?

Q: Discuss the significance of Christ reconciling with us as the example He wants us to use in reconciling with others.

Q: Read the story of the prodigal son in Luke 15:11–31 and describe how this story is an example of:
- Repentance:
- Forgiveness:
- Reconciliation:
- Rebuffed reconciliation:

Q: Personalize Luke 15:21: "I have sinned against you with my _____ (*words, thought, action*, other). Will you please forgive me?"

Q: Why would it not be advisable to reconcile with a harmful or unrepentant person?

Q: Write your own definition of the "ministry of reconciliation" including any new insight you have.

Q: To whom might God want you to be an ambassador of Christ?

Q: Pray this session will give you courage to do your part in reconciling any broken relationships.

ON YOUR OWN

Q: Who needs to hear you say Luke 15:21? Make a commitment to contact that person and confess the offense and repent.

M & M'S

Q: Do you need to personalize Luke 15:21 to each other or others? Now is the time for repentance. Help each other take action.

FACE-TO-FACE REFLECTIONS

Like forgiveness, reconciliation is a process. Dr. David Stoop and Dr. James Masteller explain the relationship of forgiveness to reconciliation in their book *Forgiving Our Parents Forgiving Ourselves*.

Face-to-Face with Euodia and Syntyche

The beauty of both forgiveness and reconciliation is that they are free actions that come from the heart. When we have wronged someone and that person has forgiven us and has opened the door of reconciliation to us, the only thing we can do is accept it.... Reconciliation requires not only mutual forgiveness but also mutual acceptance.

Acceptance is based on:

- Both parties being able to accept themselves.
- Both being willing to admit their own failures.
- Both desiring healing for the ruptured relationship.
- Both being prepared to surrender their demand for self-justification.
- Both being prepared to set aside their desire to punish the other.
- Both acknowledging that it is not easy for people to receive unconditional forgiving love.

There's always the possibility the other person will rebuff your best efforts at reconciliation. Don't let their reaction start the cycle of hurt, rejection, and anger again in your own heart. Pray God softens their heart, and keeps your heart soft. If you have the opportunity to reconcile someday—you'll be ready!

Paul's double plea in Philippians 4:2 emphasizes that Euodia and Syntyche *each* had an equal part in resolving this disagreement and reconciling. Most relationships that go through the painful process of forgiveness, repentance, and reconciliation are stronger for the effort both sides contribute to maintaining the relationship.

PERSONAL PARABLE

In my book *Praying for Your Prodigal Daughter*, I recount the story of a prodigal daughter unexpectedly calling her parents and wanting to meet.

Her sister decided not to go with us, needing to first process her feelings. I struggled...with my own feelings of hurt, anger, and fear—what would

I say? How would I react when I saw her for the first time in eight years?

The previous day at our LifeWay Chapel service, Liz Curtis Higgs, author of *Embrace Grace*...taught from Luke 15:11–32.... I thought of the father's arms open in love and acceptance as well as the other brother's resentment because he was the son who had stayed.

I clearly heard what God wanted me to do. "Just love her." I wasn't to think about the past or the pain (which I didn't think I could do) or worry about the future and if we'd get hurt again. It would be worth the risk just to love her.

While my accountability friend was again praying, God orchestrated every detail. My daughter and I both opened our arms to an incredible hug.

The future is in God's hands.... Each day I see God's love and grace a little more clearly as He repeatedly forgives and teaches me so much. He doesn't dwell on the past but just loves me today. In each situation in my life, I pray I will extend to others the same love and grace He extends to me.

* * *

Mentoring Moment

"Emphasize reconciliation, not resolution. It's unrealistic to expect everyone to agree about everything. Reconciliation focuses on the relationship, while resolution focuses on the problem. When we focus on reconciliation, the problem loses significance and often becomes irrelevant. Reconciliation means you bury the hatchet but not necessarily the issue."
—Pastor Rick Warren, *The Purpose Driven Life*

* * *

Face-to-Face with Euodia and Syntyche

Day Two

In One Accord

*P*aul seems confident Euodia and Syntyche will reconcile — work harmoniously and remain friends — if they are of one accord and *"agree with each other in the Lord"* (Philippians 4:2).

On Your Own and M&M's

Q: In Paul's opening comments in Philippians 1:1–8, note the number of times he uses *all* in reference to the church members.

Q: What do the following verses confirm about the importance of unity in the family of God?
- Psalm 133:1
- John 17:20–23
- Romans 15:5–6
- Ephesians 4:1–6

Q: Who are we first to unite with in one accord (Philippians 2:1–2)?
- What do we receive from this union?

- What do we receive from Christ's love?
- What does fellowship with the Spirit mean?

- How does verse 2 provide a pattern for relating with other believers?

Q: Philippians 4:2b in some translations reads, *"being of the same mind as the Lord."* Euodia and Syntyche probably each had thoughts about what happened between them, but they had to change their minds. Draw a line between the Scripture reference and passage.

1 Chronicles 28:9	One in heart and mind
2 Chronicles 30:12	Mind is steadfast
Isaiah 26:3	Prepare your minds for action
Acts 4:32	Willing mind
Romans 12:2	Clear minded
1 Corinthians 2:16	We have the mind of Christ
2 Corinthians 13:11	Renewing of your mind
Philippians 2:2	Like-minded
1 Peter 1:13	Be of one mind
1 Peter 4:7	Unity of mind

Q: How can believers be like-minded (Philippians 1:5–8)?

Q: Who maintains our unity (Ecclesiastes 4:12)?

ON YOUR OWN

Q: If there is disunity in your Christian relationships, what steps are you going to take to be like-minded and live in one accord?

M & M'S

Q: Talk about how to apply Ecclesiastes 4:12 to your relationship.
Q: Help each other use the wise advice in today's verses to seek the mind of Christ.
Q: Mentor, help your mentee find ways of staying in one accord with fellow believers.

FACE-TO-FACE REFLECTIONS

God calls Christians to stand united, in one accord, and in one mind with the Lord—and with each other—so we can focus on

Face-to-Face with Euodia and Syntyche

eternal kingdom work. Paul pleaded with Euodia and Syntyche to get along and reconcile for a greater cause beyond their friendship. God doesn't want us doing His work until we have His mind:

- Serving willingly with wholehearted devotion.
- Doing the Lord's work in unity.
- Sharing what we have with other believers.
- Not conforming to worldly ways, but transforming to kingdom ways.
- Testing and approving God's good, pleasing, and perfect will.
- Praying together.
- Displaying self-control.
- Living in peace.

PERSONAL PARABLE

When first leading the mentoring ministry team, I didn't realize the importance of all of us being in one accord and like-minded, until the team began disintegrating. I learned that we didn't all have to think or act alike, but we did have to share the same ministry vision and mind of Christ.

Once we were *all* on the same page spiritually and directionally, the team and the ministry flourished.

Mentoring Moment

"When we think of having the mind of Christ, we usually think in terms of getting His direction and following His will. We're focused on action. But God has a higher purpose. He is focused on character. When He gives us the mind of Jesus, He is giving us the one gift that will fundamentally alter our sinful, conflict-prone nature. It is a gift that will shape us into the very image of God."
—Chris Tiegreen, *The One Year Walk with God Devotional*, March 21

Day Three

The Bigger Picture

*I*t's essential that Christians ministering together reconcile and agree with each other in the Lord — not only for our benefit, but also for those who are watching to see how Christians deal with disagreements. The way we *work* for the Lord is a testimony and witness of the way we *live* for the Lord.

On Your Own and M&M's

Q: Read Matthew 28:18–20, The Great Commission. What does Jesus call every believer to do?

Q: How do we know that Euodia and Syntyche were not only ministry workers with Paul following the Great Commission (Philippians 1:5, *7b*, 4:3*b*), but also disciples of Christ (v. 4:3)?

Q: Philippians 4:3 (NLT) describes Euodia and Syntyche as *"these two women, for they worked hard with me in telling others the Good News."* What was the good news Paul and the ministry teams were sharing (Acts 2:38–40, 13:32–39)?
- What is the central message of Acts 2:38 and 13:38?

Q: What does Paul say the common goal of ministry workers should be (Philippians 3:10–16)?
- How do we achieve this goal (v. 13*b*)?

- Who should take the lead in pursuing the goal (v. 15a)?

- What if we think differently about the goal (v. 13b–16)?

Q: What is it called when we say one thing and do another (Philippians 1:27)?

Q: While Euodia and Syntyche were fighting, what happened to their shining star, light, and witness (Matthew 5:14–16 and Philippians 2:14–16)?

Q: How does Paul contrast those whose *citizenship is in heaven* with those who have a worldly citizenship (Philippians 3:16–20)?

- How do you see yourself walking your talk? Is your light shining? Where do onlookers see your citizenship and where do you need to improve?

Q: If you don't reconcile with another believer, what happens to your Christian witness?

M & M'S

Q: Would you characterize your M&M relationship as "a shining star in the universe"? Why or why not?

Q: If you aren't doing ministry or outreach together, pray about what God would have you do.

FACE-TO-FACE REFLECTIONS

Ministry disagreements seldom stay discreet. The fallout compromises the Lord's work, destroying the witness of "brotherly/sisterly love." This conflict is Satan's common tactic to disrupt a ministry that is changing and maturing lives or has potential to win souls.

Paul adamantly implored Euodia and Syntyche to reconcile because their arguing was working *for* Satan instead of *against* him. Likewise, when Satan has us snared in unresolved conflict — God cannot, and will not, use us for good. It's hypocrisy to preach forgiveness and remain unforgiving; to share a message of love and reconciliation with God and not do so with other believers.

Euodia and Syntyche must settle their differences and everyone needed to get back to ministry work. There was a bigger picture to consider—you can't tell others about the Prince of Peace, and be at war with one of your own. Stand firm and show God's character—joy, humility, peace, and love—and Satan retreats. But beware, he'll be back.

PERSONAL PARABLE

The founder and pastor of a large, well-known megachurch in our area, with a national television ministry, retired and transitioned the pastorate to his son. The two had a rift over the ministry direction and vision, and the son resigned. The local newspaper quoted the son's sister telling the church elders, "This is one of the most difficult times we've walked through as a family. I'm sorry that the conflict in my family has meant so much hurt to all of you."

Several of the TV ministry viewers said they "felt betrayed that the father and son couldn't put God before their family spat." Another 30-year viewer from New Jersey captured the damage: "Why can't a father and son work together for the glory of God? That's my big question."

The father and son's public conflict damaged their family and church, and also a worldwide ministry. Paul wanted to prevent this happening at the church in Philippi.

Mentoring Moment

"It is impossible for us to be united in all things in daily life, but as far as the things of the Lord are concerned, it is possible for us to submerge our petty, personal differences in order that the Lord may be magnified and His work advanced."—William MacDonald, *Believer's Bible Commentary*

Face-to-Face with Euodia and Syntyche

DAY FOUR

PRINCIPLES FOR PRACTICING PEACE

alking about forgiveness is often a major step on the way to reconciliation between two parties who have had a trust broken...For reconciliation to be complete, however, both parties need to reverse the damage that was done in the relationship, decide to give each other mercy at an occasional failure, and take active steps to build love in their relationship by valuing each other."—Everett L. Worthington Jr., *The Soul Care Bible*

ON YOUR OWN AND M&M'S

Principle One: Grieve over the injustice. In *Forgiving Our Parents Forgiving Ourselves*, Dr. David Stoop and Dr. James Mateller advise: "Mourning is therapeutic. It is healing. It is letting go of our bitterness, canceling the emotional IOUs we are holding, so that those who hurt us no longer dominate our lives as they once did." It's good to have someone with you during this process (Romans 15:15).

Q: Why is grieving the first step toward peace?
* Psalm 71:20–25
* Isaiah 61:1–4
* John 16:20

Principle Two: Replace a prideful heart with a humble heart. Chris Tiegreen warns in *The One Year Walk with God Devotional,*

August 19, "The greatest threat to peace is the pride of the human heart. It isn't content to let others be wrong about something. It feels compelled to set things straight. The result is an escalating competition to determine whose opinion will win."

Q: How can we have a humble heart that seeks peace?
- 1 Chronicles 29:17
- Psalm 4:4–5
- Psalm 13:4–6
- Psalm 51:10–13,17
- Ezekiel 36:26–28
- Daniel 4:37

Principle Three: Choose to live in peace. Ken Sande, author of *The Peacemaker: A Biblical Guide to Resolving Personal Conflict* explains: "to be reconciled means to replace hostility and separation with peace and friendship." How does the Lord value friendship?
- Job 19:19 then 42:10
- Psalm 119:63
- Proverbs 17:17
- Proverbs 18:24
- Proverbs 27:9–10
- John 15:13–15

Q: What is the Bible's advice about living in peace?
- Psalm 29:11
- Psalm 119:165
- Proverbs 3:17
- Proverbs 16:7
- Proverbs 17:1
- John 14:27
- Romans 12:18
- Romans 14:17–19

Q: How does God value the peacemakers?
- Psalm 34:14
- Psalm 37:37
- Proverbs 12:20
- Matthew 5:9
- James 3:17–18

Q: Would you say you're a peacemaker? Why or why not?

Q: How will these principles and Scriptures help you live in peace?

ON YOUR OWN

Q: If you're struggling with any of these principles to peace, ask God to bring a mentor or prayer partner into your life.

M & M'S

Q: Describe to each other a situation where you need to apply these principles to peace.
Q: If one of you is struggling with the principles, discuss the reasons and pray together that God will remove the obstacles.
Q: Mentor, take the lead in discussing the difficulties of living at peace with *everyone*.
Q: What practical steps can you both take to live peacefully within your *community of believers*?

FACE-TO-FACE REFLECTIONS

The Lord knew peaceful living would be difficult. He devoted much of the Bible to the how and why. The problem arises when a prideful heart thinks it knows best, or a shirking heart wants peace at any price. Neither is God's way.

Conflict starts in the heart. Peace principle one allows our heart to experience shock, anger, denial, despair, disappointment, and eventually, acceptance. Realizing there's no going back to change the situation frees us to go forward to change the future by our current actions (Philippians 3:13). Then we're ready for peace principle two—changing our heart. Practical ways to change our heart are:

- Stop telling the hurtful story to ourselves or anyone else.
- Speak only kind words about the offender.
- Act kindly toward the offender.
- Pray for the offender
- Give the offender a chance to repent.
- Remember your heart establishes what comes out of your mouth—peace principle three.

PERSONAL PARABLE

In her book *Generation G*, Marty Norman tells the story of practicing the three peace principles to reconcile with her stepmother, Shirley.

session five

Shirley developed Alzheimer's.... I had lost touch with her after my dad died, but my cousin George, a lawyer, advised her for many years. I suppose my neglect was partially a result of residual issues with her, due to her long-standing drinking problem. When...Shirley's Alzheimer's was rearing its ugly head...George contacted me. He needed help. Since I was the only child of my father, and since they had no children together, I was the logical one to step forward.

All peacemakers move to the front.

But would I be able to practice what I preached? Transitioning from anger and distance was not easy for me. Through much prayer and the grace of God, I was able to move forward in time toward forgiveness and caregiving.

Shirley lived a total of 11 years in an assisted living facility as well as in an Alzheimer's unit. During those years, we developed an amazing relationship.

She didn't know me the last two years, but at some level we still connected. Jim and I sat with her the day she died. We sang songs and read the Scriptures over her. She became peaceful and went faster than expected. I wished I had done more.

* * *

Mentoring Moment

"If you want God's blessing on your life and you want others to know you as a child of God, you must learn to be a peacemaker. Jesus said, *God blesses those who work for peace, for they will be called the children of God.'* Notice Jesus didn't say, 'Blessed are the peace lovers,' because everyone *loves* peace. Neither did he say, 'Blessed are the peaceable,' who are never disturbed by anything. Jesus said, 'Blessed are those who *work* for peace'—those who actively seek to resolve conflict. Peacemakers are rare because peacemaking is hard work."—Pastor Rick Warren, *The Purpose Driven Life*

* * *

Face-to-Face with Euodia and Syntyche

DAY FIVE

IT'S ALL ABOUT LOVE

"An essential means of God's Spirit working in our lives comes only in community…If we want to bear fruit in His Name, we must bear fruit together. It's the only way. He wants a unified body of Christ, not many bodies of Christ. He wants individuals to find strength in tight, durable communities." —Chris Tiegreen, *The One Year Walk with God Devotional,* September 30

ON YOUR OWN AND M&M'S

Q: Read Psalm 15. What kind of person does David say will dwell in the Lord's sanctuary and *never* be shaken?

Q: What did Paul tell these churches regarding God's will for Christians to live peacefully in community?
- Galatians 5:13–15
- Ephesians 2:13–22
- Philippians 2:3–4
- 1 Thessalonians 5:13b–18
- 1 Timothy 2:1–3,8
- Titus 3:1–9

Q: Read the salutation and greeting (first three verses) in each of his letters to the churches in 1 and 2 Corinthians, Galatians, Ephesians, Philippians, Colossians, and 1 and 2 Thessalonians. Locate the two common words and write here:
- Why do you think Paul wrote those words to *each* church?

Q: How are we to live with all men and women (Hebrews 12:14–15)?

Q: How are we to treat fellow believers?
- John 15:17
- Romans 12:9–20
- Colossians 3:12–17
- 1 Thessalonians 4:9
- 1 Peter 1:22
- 1 Peter 3:8–12
- 1 Peter 5:14

Q: What should be at the center of our Christian community (1 Corinthians 13:1–8, 13)?

Q: In what is Christian love rooted (John 3:16–17 and Philippians 1:8–11)?
- How does loving one another increase our spiritual maturity?

Q: Read Philippians 4:4–9. What words of wisdom, regarding preventing conflict and living in peaceful community, does Paul give to Euodia and Syntyche, the Philippian church, and Christians today?

- How will Paul's advice help you deal with the pressures and conflicts of life?

Q: We don't know if Euodia and Syntyche reconciled, but based on this study and Paul's exhortations to the Philippians, what ending would you put on their story?

Q: Euodia and Syntyche's legacy is an unresolved conflict made public in a letter from Paul to their church. How would it feel if your pastor announced from the pulpit that you were feuding with a fellow parishioner and that's how people remembered you?

Q: Choose what you want your legacy to be:
- ❏ She was always right, but lonely.
- ❏ She was a carrier of contagious joy.
- ❏ She nurtured many hurting friends, but never nursed a grudge.
- ❏ She had everything the world could want.
- ❏ She had few possessions, but was rich in love.
- ❏ She never started a fight, but was always fighting.
- ❏ Her words were few, but her friends were many.
- ❏ She was persuasive, but abrasive.
- ❏ She was a strong leader, but no one was following.
- ❏ She loved Jesus and others more than she loved herself!

Q: What changes, if any, do you need to make to your current legacy?

ON YOUR OWN

Q: What can you do to exemplify sisterly love in your community?

M & M'S

Q: What would you like your relationship legacy to be?

Q: How could your M&M relationship be an example of sisterly love to your Christian community?
- To the surrounding community?
- Globally?

Jesus knew the disciples' most difficult ministry issue would be relationships. His last conversations with them before going to the Cross weren't about evangelism, healing, or praying, but about loving each other and their fellow man as He had loved them, *"By this all men will know that you are my disciples, if you love one another"* (John 13:35).

In our humanness, we sever earthly relationships with believers; but Christ binds us *forever* eternally with those same believers. That's a sobering thought, isn't it? The community of Christ has no boundaries and isn't subject to our petty grievances. While we'll never reach perfection in this life, the Holy Spirit's love is continually perfecting us. Living at peace with each other is not completely up to us; we can pray that the Holy Spirit is working on the other person's heart also. When and if they're ready to reconcile, we make peace.

Is there tension or unresolved issues with a fellow believer— maybe someone you serve with in a ministry? You've both avoided the issues and when you see each other it's awkward, but neither one has been willing to work on a resolution. Now you've completed an entire study on resolving conflict and maintaining unity in the body of Christ. You know how to take the first step at peacemaking—and you know it's *your* responsibility to take that step.

Richard and Henry T. Blackaby in *Experiencing God Day-by-Day* offer a great summary of this study.

> Maybe you failed in a relationship, Jesus will not allow you to abandon it; He will help you learn from your failure and experience the difference He can make when He guides your relationships. When you try in God's strength, you may discover that success is indeed within your grasp.

Let's finish strong as peacemakers, with a legacy that reads: She was a godly woman who loved the Lord, loved her family and friends, and as much as it was up to her, got along with everyone! Then we'll be able to say with Paul, *"I have fought the good fight* [not with each other], *I have finished the race, I have kept the faith. Now there is in store for me the crown of righteousness, which the Lord, the righteous Judge, will award me on that day—and not only to me, but also to all who have longed for his appearing"* (2 Timothy 4:7–8).

PERSONAL PARABLE

I wrote this poem when God inspired me to write and speak on "From Conflict to Community."

JESUS WENT FIRST

We come from different
walks of life,
And that can sometimes
cause us strife.
He said remove the log
That has us in a fog.
Then maybe we'll see
The problem could be me.
Still we sing and take each
other's hand
And promise we will
understand.

Then a word here or there
That's not really fair.
I thought you said that,
You guessed it—a spat.

Feelings get hurt
We want to desert.
We'll just dance away,
But stop—let's pray.

We sing the songs
That say we belong
To God's family
We can't just flee.
Oh, that's hard to face.
We'd rather just race
To a friend so dear
Who will lend us an ear.

We can't avoid the conflict,
Even though it makes us
sick
To think of asking for
forgiveness.
Jesus said, "It's at my
expense."

He granted grace to you
and me.
Forgiving us so lovingly.
The undeserving and the
worst,
He didn't ask us to go first.

Mentoring Moment

"The Christian life is a loving life. An unloving life is not Christian.
Let love, above all else, define you."
—Chris Tiegreen, *The One Year Walk with God Devotional*

"Don't waste time bothering whether you 'love your neighbor;
act as if you did. As soon as we do this, we find one of the great
secrets. When you are behaving as if you loved someone, you will
presently come to love him."—C. S. Lewis

• • •

FAITH IN ACTION

What from this session does God want you to apply today?

LET'S PRAY TOGETHER

*Lord, You showed us the way to love others and to live a life of peace.
Forgive us the times we've bought into the world's ways and not followed Your model of love and reconciliation. We want to be women
whose lives lead others to You by the peace they see in our hearts
and our actions. Let us not be anxious, but let our light shine so the
world can see that it is possible to live at peace when we choose to
agree in the Lord. Amen.*

I joined the Woman to Woman Mentoring Ministry when I was a baby Christian stay-at-home mom, 7 months pregnant, with a 3-year-old son and an unbelieving husband. My mother died when I was 14, and I never had another mother role model. I didn't have Christian friends or know the Christian walk, but I knew I needed to change. I felt empty, with no purpose in my life.

I received a call from my mentor. She was older and an empty-nester. I told her about my struggles, and we seemed to hit it off. I couldn't believe God gave her to me. It was a perfect match. *I thought.* But as weeks went by, I hardly saw her.

I was disappointed and angry. Why would God give her to me if she wasn't going to be around? I thought she was supposed to help direct me. When we did talk, it seemed I mentored her more than she mentored me. This wasn't what I had expected or wanted!

As time passed, I felt drawn to other women in the mentoring ministry and began serving. I heard how God worked in the M&M relationships and how new friendships were formed, but I didn't feel jealous they had what I desperately wanted. I was happy for them.

Looking back, I see God's bigger plan. My relationship with my mentor was two-sided: I helped her; she helped me. Maybe if she had been more available, I wouldn't have been as active in the ministry or met so many other wonderful Christian women. I was using my gifts and talents to help further God's kingdom, and I was growing in my walk with the Lord. I learned the importance of community: how we can do mighty things for God together.

It's amazing how God works through us. I now mentor new moms and new Christians, and I have a heart for women who have lost their moms. I can take all I've learned and apply it to my daily walk and show other women the things God has taught me.

CLOSING
MATERIALS

Christian Community Begins

We Conclude Our Study of Euodia and Syntyche

Let's Pray a Closing Prayer Together

Father, You know the areas that cause us to harden our heart. Please remove those stumbling blocks from our lives and replace them with peace, love, patience, kindness, and humility. Open our eyes to see where we have unresolved conflict and help us take steps to reconcile. Where have we avoided a person or an area of service in ministry because of a personality conflict or dislike for someone? Father, help us to love our fellow man and woman — to think more highly of others than we do ourselves — to live by Your ways and not our own or the world's ways. Help us not to feel we always must be right or justified, but to be tolerant of others' ideas. Help us forgive others as You have forgiven us, Lord. We want to be worthy of Your forgiveness and to be able to forgive others 70 times 7. Remove any scorekeeping or tape playing in our minds. Give us a love that passes all understanding…especially our own. Father, we want to be like You in every way, and we know that how we handle this area of our life could be a positive or a negative witness. We can do all things through You who gives us strength. Amen.

Congratulations! You've just completed a study that I know wasn't easy. I hope you have learned biblical skills and feel encouraged and ready to make a conscious effort to be the first to apologize, swallow rebuttals that come into your throat, and wherever it is possible and up to you, to live at peace with everyone.

You might want to print the "7 Biblical Steps to Resolving Conflict" on pages 71–72 and keep them in your Bible, purse, day-timer, or all three! Also memorize Matthew 5:23–24 and 18:15–17 and use these verses to guide you in confronting conflict.

The purpose of this study was to help you delve into God's Word and learn for yourself what He has to say about resolving conflict and living in community. There also are many great Christian books written on the topic of conflict resolution. If you would like to read more on the topic, here are a few suggestions.

- *The Peacemaker: A Biblical Guide to Resolving Personal Conflict* by Ken Sande (Baker Books, 2004).
- *Forgiving Our Parents Forgiving Ourselves* by Dr. David Stoop and Dr. James Masteller (Servant Publications, 2004).
- *Leading Women Who Wound: Strategies for an Effective Ministry* by Sue Edwards & Kelley Mathews (Moody Publishers, 2009).
- *In the Company of Women* by Brenda Hunter, PhD (Multnomah Books, 2006).
- *Overcoming Emotions that Destroy: Practical Help for Those Angry Feelings* by Chip Ingram and Dr. Becca Johnson (Baker Books, 2009).
- *Murder by Family: The Incredible True Story of a Son's Treachery and a Father's Forgiveness* by Kent Whitaker (Howard Books, 2008). Read the complete story of a modern-day prodigal.
- *Gone in a Heartbeat: Our Daughters Died...Our Faith Endures* by David & Marie Works with Dean Merrill (Tyndale House Publishers, Inc., 2009). A true and heart wrenching story of amazing forgiveness and reconciliation in the body of Christ.
- *Praying for Your Prodigal Daughter: Hope, Help, & Encouragement for Hurting Parents* by Janet Thompson (Howard Books/Simon & Schuster, 2008). Read the miraculous story of praying home

my prodigal daughter, Kim. I also offer encouragement and tips to help parents of prodigals pray for their daughters.

- *Dear God, They Say It's Cancer: A Companion Guide for Women on the Breast Cancer Journey* by Janet Thompson (Howard Books/ Simon & Schuster, 2006). My opportunity to mentor other breast-cancer sisters from my own journey.

- *Woman to Woman Mentoring How to Start, Grow, and Maintain A Mentoring Ministry DVD Leader Kit* is available at your local LifeWay bookstore or at www.lifeway.com or by calling 1-800-458-2772.

- Additional "Face-to-Face" Bible Studies:
  Face-to-Face with Mary and Martha: Sisters in Christ
  Face-to-Face with Naomi and Ruth: Together for the Journey
  Face-to-Face with Elizabeth and Mary: Generation to Generation

To learn more about AHW Ministries, Janet's writing and speaking ministry, visit www.womantowomanmentoring.com.

LEADER'S GUIDE

FOR GROUP-STUDY FACILITATORS AND M&M'S

SUGGESTIONS FOR FACILITATORS

Congratulations! God has appointed you the awesome privilege of setting the pace and focus for this group. Regardless of how many groups you have facilitated, this group will be a new and unique experience. This guide's suggestions and tips have helped me, and I trust they also will benefit you. Change or adapt them as you wish, but they are a solid place to start.

ORGANIZING THE SESSIONS

Small groups generally meet in a home, and larger churchwide groups usually meet at the church or other facility. I suggest for the larger group that you form small groups by sitting everyone at round tables. Appoint or ask for a volunteer facilitator for each table and have the group sit together for the five sessions of this study. Then both small-group leaders and large-group table facilitators can use the following format.

1. **Starting the sessions** — In my experience, members usually come in rushed, harried, and someone is always late — creating the perplexing dilemma of when to start. I suggest beginning on time because you are committed to ending on time. Don't wait for the last late person to arrive. Waiting dishonors those who arrive on time and sets the precedent that it's OK to be a little late because "they won't start without me, anyway." Also, if you delay the start time, you may not finish the discussion.

2. **Icebreakers** — Each session has an "icebreaker" that is fun, interactive, helps the group become acquainted, and encourages on-time arrivals. It's an interactive activity participants won't want to miss. The icebreaker also eases group members out of their hectic day and into a study mode.

3. **Format** — Each session includes: Opening Prayer, Icebreaker, Five Days of Selected Discussion Questions, Prayer, Fellowship.

4. **The Session Guide provides you with:**
- Preparation: what you need to do or obtain in advance.
- Icebreakers: openers for each meeting.
- Bold: the action you need to say or take.
- Ideas: to help facilitate discussion and suggest answers that might be less obvious.
- Session name, day, and page number: to identify area discussed.

5. **Suggested time** — Each session has nine numbered activities. Fifteen minutes on each number equals a two-hour meeting. This is a guideline to modify according to your time allotment. Let the Holy Spirit guide you and cover what seems applicable and pertinent to your group.

6. **Facilitating discussion** — Questions and Scriptures to discuss are only a suggestion to enhance what participants have studied on their own already. Feel free to cover whatever material you think or the group feels is pertinent. Think about ways to:
- Keep all engaged in conversation.
- Avoid "rabbit trails."
- Assure each one has a clear understanding of the points under discussion.
- Encourage members to stay accountable by doing their lesson and arriving on time.

Big job you say! You can do it with God's help and strength.

7. **Prayertime** — Prayer should be an ongoing and vital part of your group. Open and close your times together in prayer. There is a prayer at the end of each session to pray together. Taking prayer requests can often get lengthy and be a source of gossip, if not handled properly. Let me share with you a way that works well in groups:
- At the end of the meeting, give each woman an index card and instruct her to write *one* prayer request pertaining to the study and pass the card to the leader/facilitator. Mix up the cards and have each person pick one. If someone picks her own card, have her put it back in the pile and pick a different one.
- When everyone has a card, go around the group (or table) and each person is to read the name and prayer request on her card

so others can write down the requests. Participants may want to use the Prayer & Praise Journal starting on page 139.

- Instruct the group to hold hands and agree in unison as each participant prays the prayer request for the person whose card she has. This allows everyone to experience praying.
- Each woman takes home the card she received and prays for that person, ongoing.
- As the leader/facilitator, pray between meetings for the group, your leadership, and ask God to mentor you and the members. And have fun!

8. **Communion**—You will offer communion during the last session (assuming doing so creates no problems in your church context). Remind the group that taking communion together as believers is significant and unifying in three ways, by:

- proclaiming the Lord's death,
- providing an opportunity for fellowship and unity, and
- giving participants an occasion for remembrance of Jesus.

If there are nonbelievers, explain that communion is for believers. This is a perfect opportunity to ask if they would like to accept Jesus Christ as their Savior and pray the Salvation Prayer on page 32. If they are not ready, then ask them to sit quietly while the believers take communion. Ask someone to read aloud the Scriptures in Matthew 26:26–29 or Luke 22:14–20 and have the group partake of the juice and bread at the appropriate spot in the Scripture reading. Matthew 26:30 says, *"When they had sung a hymn they went out to the Mount of Olives."* Close the time of communion with a worship song.

9. **Fellowship time**—It's important for relationships to develop so group members feel comfortable sharing during discussions. A social time with refreshments provides a nice way to bring closure to the evening and allows time to chat. Encourage everyone to stay. Fellowship is part of the small group experience and allows larger groups to get to know other members.

M & M'S

Use the Session Guide for additional information and help in determining which questions to emphasize during meetings.

SESSION GUIDE

SESSION ONE—THEIR STORY

- **Bring** a CD player and a Gilbert and Sullivan CD available in music stores or online at www.music.com.
- **Provide** a whiteboard and felt-tip marker. **Make** two vertical columns on the whiteboard and **title** one Reasons We Avoid Conflict and the other Consequences of Unresolved Conflict.

1. **Opening Prayer: Hold hands** as a group and **open** in prayer.
2. **Icebreaker: Can You Relate?**—Beautiful Music but No Harmony

♦ **Have** everyone relax and listen as you play a short musical selection of Gilbert and Sullivan.

Q: **Ask:** What did it feel like listening to this beautiful music, knowing the estranged relationship of the composers?

3. **Day One: How Does Euodia and Syntyche's Story Relate to Us?, Page 16**

Q: **Ask:** How many of you had read the Book of Philippians before doing this study?

Q: **Ask:** Had anyone ever noticed Euodia and Syntyche in verses 4:2–3 or heard of these two women?

♦ **Discuss** the Scriptures they noted that support Paul wrote the Book of Philippians to address the dispute between Euodia and Syntyche.

Q: **Ask** several volunteers to read Acts 16:11–15, 40. **Discuss** the scene in Acts compared to Philippians 4:2–3.

Q: **Ask** someone to read Proverbs 18:19 and **lead a discussion** of how the verse applies to Gilbert and Sullivan and Euodia and Syntyche.

Q: **Ask:** How many of you like conflict?

Q: **Ask:** Who has an unresolved conflict in your life right now? **Invite** anyone who wants to share, **advising** not to disclose names or situations everyone would recognize.

Q: **Then ask:** Who has ended a relationship over an unresolved conflict and another time worked through a disagreement and maintained the relationship? **Ask:** What was the difference between the two scenarios?

♦ One of these questions probably will apply to everyone, so **state**: It's easy to see that Euodia and Syntyche's story applies to all of us.

4. **Day Two: Differences of Opinion Can Be Normal and Healthy, Page 19**

Q: **Ask** if considering conflict as a normal and healthy part of life was a new concept? **Discuss** responses.

Q: **Read** 1 Corinthians 12:4–11. **Ask:** Even though God made us each unique, what is identical in every believer's life? (Answer: The Holy Spirit)

Q: **Ask:** Why don't all Christians have identical opinions?

Q: **Ask** several to read aloud Philippians 2:1–2 and 3:12–15. **Ask:** In what areas should mature Christians think alike?

Q: **Read** Proverbs 27:17. **Ask:** What describes a healthy disagreement and when can it bring positive change? (Possible answers: Fair debates can lead to breakthroughs in science, changing the status quo, and introducing new innovative ideas.)

♦ **Ask** if anyone has a Proverbs 27:17 person in her life and how does it help.

5. **Day Three: When are Differences of Opinion Unhealthy?, Page 22**

Q: **Ask:** When are differences of opinion among Christians unhealthy?

Q: **Ask** what they learned from each of the verses on "divisiveness among Christians."

Q: **Discuss** fertile grounds for disunity and conflict in the church and in all relationships.

Q: **Read** Luke 11:17. **Ask:** Do any of you have divisions on issues with other believers?

♦ **Encourage** them that this study will help with learning how to resolve those issues.

Q: **Discuss** Luke 12:51, and **ask** if being a Christian has caused division among family or friends.

Q: **Ask:** What does this statement mean to you? "Believers don't need *unanimity* in everything, but we do need *unity* in working for the Lord."

6. **Day Four: Conflict Avoidance, Page 25**

Q: **Ask:** What were the rewards of Paul confronting the Corinthians? (Answer: Repentance, even though it was a hard letter for him to write and them to receive.)

♦ **Discuss** Paul and the Corinthians, and Janet and her neighbor, as examples that all confrontations don't have to result in conflict, but can actually help avoid it.

Q: **Ask:** What should be our attitude when we confront someone? (Answer: loving, respectful, and letting God do the changing)

Q: **Ask:** What are terms and other applications for *confront* that don't imply conflict? Examples: face, deal with, talk to, encounter, or a phrase like "confront my overeating issues."

Q: **Ask:** How should we receive wise council or constructive criticism?

Q: **Ask** for reasons women avoid confronting conflict. **Have** someone list on the whiteboard under "Reason We Avoid Conflict."

Q: **Ask** if anyone identifies with these reasons, and **discuss** ways women avoid conflict.

7. **Day Five: Consequences of Unresolved Conflict, Page 29**

Q: **Discuss** potential negative consequences of ministry workers Euodia and Syntyche's unresolved conflict?

Q: **Ask:** What does Paul call the Corinthians in his first letter to them? (Answer: infants in Christ)

♦ **Ask:** If the Corinthians were spiritually mature, what would they remember? (Answer: They were all fellow workers for Christ with a task of spreading the gospel.)

Q: **Ask** someone to read the list of the sinful nature from Galatians 5:19–21. **Discuss** that there's no graded difference between the sin of discord among believers and immorality.

Q: **Ask:** How can we counter our naturally sinful nature? (Answer: the fruit of the Spirit)

♦ **Go back** to the whiteboard and make a list of the "Consequences of Unresolved Conflict."

Q: **Ask** if anyone made a decision for Christ during this session, or if anyone would like to do that right now. If you have new believers, congratulate them and celebrate.

8. **Prayertime** (See Leader's Guide, p. 123.)
   Prayer request, prayer partner exchange, and group prayer.

9. **Fellowship and Refreshments**

- **Provide** a whiteboard with two different colored markers.
- **Divide** the whiteboard into two columns. **Use** a different color for each side and **title** the columns: Trigger Gossip Words/ Phrases and Lovingly Change the Subject.

1. **Opening Prayer: Hold** hands as a group and **open** in prayer.
2. **Icebreaker: Divide** into two groups according to those who identified with the personality styles suggested on page 36–37 for Euodia or Syntyche.

♦ **Instruct** each group to select a spokeswoman to present the group's collective responses. You, the leader, **act** as moderator, and if necessary, mediator.

♦ **Give** them a hypothetical scenario: The Women's Ministry team has agreed to prayerfully fast sugar together every Wednesday for the work of the ministry. There's a disagreement: The Euodia group maintains fruit isn't a sugar and is OK to eat on fasting Wednesday. The Syntyche group says fruit is sugar and isn't allowed. Each side is adamant and unyielding in their opinion.

♦ **Give** them about 5 minutes to develop reasons to defend their side on this issue, then **reconvene. Have** each spokeswoman present her group's case in the form of a debate.

Q: As moderator, **ask both sides:** What is the common goal of fasting together?

Q: **Ask** what sins they might fall into if they remain divided on this issue.

♦ **Let** the "audience" **discuss** that arguing over the fruit issue thwarts the common goal of the fast.

♦ **Have** them stay in the E&S groups with their championed opinions on this topic and personality type. **Use** the fasting scenario throughout the rest of the session.

2. **Day One: What Do We Fight About?, Page 35**

Q: **Ask:** What do you think Euodia and Syntyche were arguing about?

Q: **Ask:** What is at the root of the speculative conflict issues. (Some answers: pride, jealousy, coveting, spiritual immaturity, thinking your agenda is the most important, poor communication)

Q: **Ask** each E&S group what's at the root of their conflict with the other group.

Q: **Ask**: How can having a God-given unique purpose cause conflict?

Q: **Read** Romans 12:3. **Ask**: what counters many of the roots of conflict? (Answer: Don't think of yourselves more highly than anyone else. Each created with a purpose. Help each other achieve their goals and look out for each other.)

Q: **Ask:** Whose purpose should prevail? (Answer: God's)

4. **Day Two: I Want My *Own* Way, Page 38**

Q: **Ask:** What is at the core of fear? (Answer: self-preservation and pride)

Q: **Ask:** What is at the center of wanting your own way? (Answer: pride)

Q: **Ask:** How does God feel about wrongful or self-centered pride?

Q: **Ask** a few to share their definition of pride.

◆ **Discuss** Paul's advice for countering pride in Philippians 2:3–8 and Peter's in 1 Peter 5:5–6.

Q: **Ask:** How did Jesus resist Satan? (Answer: Scripture)

Q: **Read** Ephesians 6:10–18. **Ask:** How can we stand firm against the enemy?

Q: **Ask:** How hard is it to remain humble?

◆ Who is our example of humility? (Answer: Jesus)

◆ Who wants to prevent you from developing humility? (Answer: Satan)

Q: **Ask:** How did jealousy devastate the relationship between Joseph and his brothers?

Q: **Ask:** How does Romans 13:8–10 and Galatians 6:4 say we can overcome coveting/jealousy?

Q: **Have** members from each E&S group read the Scriptures on page 29 and tell the wise counsel of how to avoid entanglement in jealousy, coveting, and envy.

Q: **Discuss** how today's lesson encouraged them to be more humble and not want their own way.

5. **Day Three: You Make Me So Angry!, Page 43**

Q: **Divide** the Scriptures on anger on page 43 between the E&S groups. **Have** each group discuss how their assigned Scriptures could apply if they become angry over the fasting disagreement.

Q: **Ask:** When would anger be appropriate?

Q: **Divide** the Scriptures on bitterness page 44 between each group and **have** them discuss how their anger could turn to the sin of bitterness.

Q: **Reconvene** and **ask:** What action does Ephesians 4:31–32 say will rid us of anger and bitterness?

Q: **Ask** the "outies" and "inies" to raise their hand and note any correlation to their E&S group.

♦ **Discuss** the best balance between the two expressions of anger by going over the ABCD steps on page 45.

6. **Day Four: Have You Heard?, Page 47**

Q: **Discuss** James 3:2–12 and the power of words. **Ask:** Why do we all struggle with misspoken words?

Q: **Ask:** What new respect do you have for words?

Q: **Ask:** Where does our propensity for speaking unrighteous words start? (Answer: our heart)

♦ **Read** Psalm 119:11. **Ask:** How can we change what comes out of our heart?

Q: **Ask:** What should we do before we speak? (Answer: stop and pray)

♦ **Discuss** their ideas on how to remember to pray before speaking.

Q: **Ask:** How might each E&S group start gossiping to others about their point of view. **Discuss** how gossip turns to slander.

Q: **Read** Titus 2:3–5 and **discuss** the role of spiritually older women.

Q: **Ask:** What can be the biggest source of gossip among Christians? (Answer: praying together and public prayer requests)

Q: **Discuss** their Trigger Gossip Words/Phrases and how to Lovingly Change the Subject. **Have** someone write them on the whiteboard.

7. **Day Five: Unmet Expectations, Page 52**

Q: **Have** someone read the story in Matthew 20:1–16. **Ask:** What did you learn about expectations and comparing ourselves to others?

Q: **Ask:** What's your natural inclination when someone betrays or wrongs you?

♦ **Ask:** How could acting on these inclinations affect your witness?

Q: **Read** Luke 6:33–35. **Discuss** the reward for lowering expectations and releasing our "rights"?

Q: **Have** the E&S groups **discuss** within their group the story of Linda LeSourd Lader in the Personal Parable on 33. **Instruct** them to discuss how "locking the door" on separation and division between the E&S groups will encourage them to work on resolving the fasting conflict.

◆ **Bring** the group back together and **ask** the spokeswomen to report their group's discussion. **Advise** the E&S groups that they'll work on ideas for resolving the conflict next time you meet.

8. **Prayertime**

◆ Personalize and pray together Matthew 6:10.

◆ Prayer request, prayer partner exchange, and group prayer.

9. **Fellowship and Refreshments**

SESSION THREE—AGREEING IN THE LORD

● **Provide** blank index cards.

1. Opening Prayer: **Hold** hands as a group and **open** in prayer.

2. Icebreaker: **Have** the group go into their E&S groups from session two.

◆ **Pass out** index cards and **instruct** each woman to write on the card something unusual about herself that others in the group might not know about her. **Have** everyone turn the cards back into you by group.

◆ **Distribute** the cards to members of the opposite group. If the groups do not have an even number of people, you take a card and/or keep a card within a group, but instruct the owner not to identify her card.

◆ **Give** the groups about 5 minutes to decide who they think each card belongs to, and then bring them all back together and have fun seeing if they guessed right.

3. **Day One: What's a Christian to Do?**, Page 57

Q: **Ask** someone to read aloud Matthew 18:15–17, and **discuss** the biblical protocol of dealing with conflict. Then **go through** the steps with the E&S groups.

◆ Step 1. **Have** the Euodia spokeswoman approach the Syntyche spokeswoman, but **instruct** them not to reach an agreement. Each spokeswoman consults with her group as to what to say.

◆ Step 2. You **act** as a mediator and help the spokeswomen try to reach a suitable solution that will appease both sides and allow them to reconcile, but not necessarily give in. They agree to disagree. **Let** the groups be creative in this and see if they can do it.

Q: **Ask** what the 3rd step is if they don't agree after meeting with the mediator.

Q: **Discuss** how Paul applied Matthew 18:15–17 to the conflict between Euodia and Syntyche.

◆ **Discuss** what it means to "agree in the Lord."

Q: **Ask** for their definition of "mediate." **Ask:** Who does 1 Timothy 2:5 say is the mediator between God and us? (Answer: Jesus)

◆ **Discuss** where to find a Christian mediator.

4. Day Two: The Power of an Apology, Page 61

Q: **Ask:** Why do you think Euodia and Syntyche hadn't already apologized to each other?

Q: **Ask:** How did God respond when he was unjustifiably wronged? (Answer: abounding in love, forgiveness, compassion, slow to anger)

Q: **Ask:** How does God want us responding when we feel wronged or when we wrong others?

◆ **Discuss** their reasons for why it's so hard to offer an apology and why we want to be right.

◆ **Ask** what would make an apology easier: (Answer: prayer and following Jesus's example)

Q: **Ask:** What is the purpose of an apology? (Answer: reconciliation)

◆ **Discuss** Zander's advice on apologizing in the Face-to-Face Reflections on page 63.

Q: **Ask** each E&S group spokeswoman to apologize to the other spokeswoman for_____ (have each group fill in the blank) without minimizing or defending their position.

5. Day Three: Choose Your Mountains, Page 65

Q: **Ask** someone to read Philippians 1:15–18, and **discuss** Paul's position regarding those who were trying to stir up trouble for him. **Be sure** they arrive at the conclusion: If they're spreading the truth of the gospel…what does it matter?

Q: **Discuss** Nehemiah's response to angry opponents trying to discourage him, and Billy Graham's comments in the Mentoring Moment on page 67.

Q: **Go back** into E&S groups and **instruct** them to discuss and report whether this team division over fasting was avoidable. Was it a mountain worth climbing? **Remember** there's no right or wrong answer, depending on how critical each side sees the issue.

6. **Day Four: Agreeing to Disagree, Page 68**

Q: **Reconvene** and **discuss** how Paul first handled his disagreement with Barnabas and Mark and then how he talked kindly about them later.

♦ **Ask:** How do you think Paul's spiritual maturity influenced his later agreeing to disagree and reconcile with fellow workers for Christ?

Q: **Ask** if anyone would like to share how maturing in her faith has helped her deal with conflict.

Q: **Have** each E&S group discuss among themselves if they're ready to agree to disagree with the other group (providing there's still a division of thought). **See if** the spokeswomen can have that discussion without it escalating back into an argument.

7. **Day Five: 7 Biblical Steps to Resolving Conflict, Page 71**

Q: **Explain** a new conflict scenario to the E&S groups: there's extra money in the ministry budget and the Euodia group wants to throw an appreciation party for all the ministry workers. The Syntyche group wants to start a ministry library. **Give** the two groups time to discuss their issue.

Q: **Practice** going through "7 Biblical Steps to Resolving Conflict" with the budget disagreement:

♦ The E&S group spokeswomen do the talking.

♦ The Euodia spokeswoman initiates step one, setting up a meeting with the Syntyche spokeswoman.

♦ Then **have** them go through the "7 Biblical Steps to Resolving Conflict." **Be sure** they start and end with prayer.

8. **Prayertime**

♦ Prayer request, prayer partner exchange, and group prayer.

9. **Fellowship and Refreshments**

● **Bring** a large inflated balloon or a lightweight beach ball.

1. **Opening Prayer: Hold** hands as a group and **open** in prayer.

2. **Icebreaker: Tell** the group that you're going to **toss** the balloon or ball into the air towards them, and whoever receives it is to say a myth about forgiveness and toss the balloon to someone else who will say the countering truth. **Keep** the balloon/ball going until they cover all the forgiveness myths and truths in day three on page 85.

3. **Day One: We Forgive Because We Were Forgiven, Page 76**

Q: **Discuss** what each Scripture on page 76 says about the conditions of receiving God's unconditional forgiveness. What are we to do?

Q: **Read** John 20:21–23 and **discuss** our role in encouraging people to accept God's forgiveness? **Be sure** they understand that *we* can't grant others God's forgiveness for their sins, only God can do that. But we can help others understand how to confess their sins to God and pray to receive His forgiveness. Our example and witness can be either good or bad, depending on how we handle forgiveness ourselves.

Q: **Ask:** What does Luke 7:47 say is evidence that God forgave us? (Answer: we love much)

Q: **Talk** about Corrie ten Boom forgiving the cruel prison guard and her comment about other victims of Nazi brutality, who were able to forgive, were best able to rebuild their lives.

Q: **Ask:** How can the Mentoring Moment quote by Pastor Tim Westcott on page 79 help you keep in perspective forgiving others, and why God's forgiveness means we need to forgive others?

4. **Day Two: Mercy and Grace, Page 80**

Q: **Assign** one of the E&S groups the verses on the "gospel of God's grace," and the other group the verses warning about a resentful, revengeful, unforgiving heart on page 80. **Give** them a few moments to discuss then **reconvene** and **ask** the spokeswomen to summarize what their verses said.

Q: **Ask** if they had ever considered that not forgiving someone could possibly cause that person to miss God's grace.

Q: **Read** John 1:14 and **ask** what it means to be full of grace *and* truth.

◆ **Ask:** do you err on the side of excusing or legalism?

Q: **Read** Proverbs 29:26. **Ask:** Do you trust God's sovereignty for justice?

Q: **Ask** some to share their definitions of truth, justice, mercy, and grace.

Q: **Ask** what Buechner's opening quote means to them.

Q: **Discuss** the amazing forgiveness of Kent Whitaker in the excerpts from *Murder by Family*.

5. **Day Three: Myths and Truths, Page 84**

Q: **Ask:** What is the main difference between forgive and reconcile? **Be sure** they arrive at forgiveness is unilateral — only takes one person and is between that person and God. Reconciliation is bilateral — requiring the cooperation of both parties and is between them both.

Q: **Discuss** any forgiveness myths they believed.

Q: **Read** John 8:31–32. **Ask:** How has learning the truths about forgiveness set you free to forgive?

6. **Day Four: Knowing How to Forgive, Page 88**

Q: **Ask** what they learned from the Scriptures on page 88 about how to forgive like God forgives.

Q: **Ask:** What's the Lord full of that He can easily forgive us? (Answer: compassion, love, mercy)

Q: **Ask** if they feel that showing mercy and compassion would help them forgive easier.

Q: **Ask** someone to read 2 Corinthians 2:5–11. **Discuss** the steps of forgiving a Christian who sins and repents.

Q: **Discuss** the REACH steps of forgiveness on page 89–90.

◆ **Ask** if anyone has experience using these steps to forgiveness — even if they didn't realize they were doing it, as Janet discussed in the Personal Parable about forgiving her mother.

7. **Day Five: Unconditional Forgiveness, Page 91**

Q: **Have** someone read the story of the unforgiving servant in Matthew 18:23–35. **Ask:** How sincere must our forgiveness be?

Q: **Discuss** Joseph unconditionally forgiving his brothers. **Ask** if anyone thinks she could do that?

Q: **Ask** if they feel God unconditionally forgave and forgot their sins? **Ask:** Is it hard to believe that God could forgive some of the things you've done?

- ♦ **Discuss** why it's impossible to forgive unconditionally if you don't believe that you are forgiven yourself. **Use** as a reference the story from the movie on page 93 in the Face-to-Face Reflections.
- ♦ Before going into your time of prayer, **note** if you see anyone hesitating, and **stop** and **pray** if someone needs to be reassured of God's forgiveness.
- Q: **Ask** if anyone wants prayer for someone she needs to unconditionally forgive, either now, or from the past. **Assure** them that even if the person is dead, they still can forgive them.
- **8. Prayertime**
- ♦ Prayer request, prayer partner exchange, and group prayer.
- **9. Fellowship and Refreshments.**

SESSION FIVE–FROM CONFLICT TO COMMUNITY
- ● **Obtain** lined sheet paper for everyone.
- ● **Bring** a DVD player and a CD of the song, "Shine" by Matt Redman. For more information about the song go to www.mattredman.com, and for the lyrics www.allthelyrics.com/lyrics/matt_redman/.
- ● Or www.youtube.com/watch?v=G7WyCK-HmVs you can play on a computer or iPod. Philippians 2:15 was the inspiration for "Shine."
- **1. Opening Prayer: Hold** hands as a group and **open** in prayer.
- **2. Icebreaker: Go back** into the E&S groups. **Give** each group a sheet of lined paper and **ask** them to write the "Top 10 Good Results" if the relationship between the two groups went from conflict over the fasting or budgeting issues and back to community and working together as a team.
- ♦ **Have** the other group write the "Top 10 Bad Results" if the two groups remained in conflict. **Give** them about 10 minutes, and then **reconvene. Have** the groups switch lists and the spokeswoman from each group reads the other group's list.
- **3. Day One: The Ministry of Reconciliation, Page 97**
- Q: **Ask:** What does it mean to be an "ambassador for Christ?"
- ♦ **Ask** if they realize that they're either good or bad ambassadors for Christ every day!
- Q: **Read** 2 Corinthians 5:18–21 and **discuss.**

Q: **Read** Matthew 5:23–24. **Ask:** While Euodia and Syntyche were fighting, what gifts would God not want from them: (Suggestions: time, money, ministry)

♦ **Discuss** how this passage applies to their E&S group arguments and to them personally.

Q: **Have** someone read Luke 15:11–31. **Discuss** how the story of the prodigal son is an example of: repentance, forgiveness, reconciliation, and rebuffed reconciliation.

♦ **Have** each E&S group say to the other: "I have sinned against you with my _____ (fill in the blank). Will you please forgive me?"

♦ **Ask** if anyone needs to say this to someone in her personal life.

Q: **Ask** several to share their definition of the "ministry of reconciliation."

♦ **Discuss** if they had thought of reconciliation as a ministry.

♦ **Discuss** the concept of mutual acceptance and repntance being necessary for reconciliation on page 98–99.

4. **Day Two: In One Accord,** Page 101

Q: **Discuss** the verses regarding unity in the family of God.

Q: **Discuss** the significance of Christians *being like-minded, being of the same mind as the Lord,* and *being in one accord.*

Q: **Discuss** what the matching Scriptures on page 102 teach about having the mind of Christ.

Q: **Ask:** How does having the mind of Christ change our attitude and lead to unity of believers?

Q: **Ask** the two E&S groups to talk about how they can apply like-mindedness to their fasting and budget conflict issues and achieve unity again in their team?

5. **Day Three: The Bigger Picture, Page 104**

Q: **Read** Matthew 28:18–20. **Ask** what part they have in The Great Commission.

Q: **Discuss** churches', Paul's, and Euodia and Syntyche's ministry of telling others about God's forgiveness through Jesus Christ.

Q: **Read** Philippians 3:10–16. **Ask:** what should be the common goal of both E&S group's ministry?

Q: **Ask:** If the E&S groups continue arguing over fasting, budgeting and other issues, but try telling people how much God loves and forgives them, what is that called? (Answer: hypocrisy)

Q: **Read:** Matthew 5:14–16 and Philippians 2:14–16. **Ask:** how does hypocrisy affect your witness, your light in a dark world, and the integrity of your life and ministry?

♦ **Discuss** what probably will happen to the ministry of the E&S groups if they don't reconcile.

Q: **Have** each E&S group meet together and decide which is most important to them: being right or the purpose for which they were fasting—the ministry? Being right or being good stewards of God's money?

6. Day Four: Principles for Practicing Peace, Page 107

Q: **Stay** in the E&S groups and **instruct** them to go through the three principles of peace and the Scriptures and decide if they're going to choose peace with the other group.

Q: **Reconvene** and **ask** who in each group sees themselves as a peacemaker and why. **Ask** how the others will live in peace.

7. Day Five: It's All About Love, Page 111

Q: **Discuss** the verses on page 111 regarding God's will for Christians to serve together in peaceful community.

Q: **Assign** reading of the verses on how to treat fellow believers.

Q: **Read** John 3:16–17 and Philippians 1:8–11. **Ask:** What is love rooted in? (Answer: Christ)

Q: **Have** the Euodia team read Philippians 4:4–9, and Syntyche team read Colossians 3:12–17.

♦ **Ask** each team how these verses will help prevent similar disagreements in the future?

Q: **Conclude** with each woman saying what she wants her legacy to be.

8. Prayertime

♦ **Review** the answers to prayer they have seen during this study.

♦ **Take** communion together (see p. 124).

♦ **Have** everyone read together Philippians 2:14–15.

♦ **Turn** the lights out and **burn** one candle. **Play** the song "Shine" and sing along.

♦ **Read** the closing prayer on page 119 together.

9. Fellowship and Refreshments.

♦ **Talk** about the study the group wants to do next. See page 144 for additional "Face-to-Face" Bible studies.

Face-to-Face with Euodia and Syntyche

Prayer & Praise Journal

Prayer & Praise Journal

Prayer & Praise Journal

Prayer & Praise Journal

New Hope® Publishers is a division of WMU®, an international organization that challenges Christian believers to understand and be radically involved in God's mission. For more information about WMU, go to www.wmu.com. More information about New Hope books may be found at www.newhopepublishers.com. New Hope books may be purchased at your local bookstore.

If you've been blessed by this book, we would like to hear your story. The publisher and author welcome your comments and suggestions at: newhopereader@wmu.org

Other New Hope Bible Studies for Women

Face-to-Face with Mary and Martha	Face-to-Face with Naomi and Ruth	Face-to-Face with Elizabeth and Mary
Sisters in Christ	*Together for the Journey*	*Generation to Generation*
Janet Thompson	Janet Thompson	Janet Thompson
ISBN-10: 1-59669-254-5	ISBN-10: 1-59669-253-7	ISBN-10: 1-59669-252-9
ISBN-13: 978-1-59669-254-1	ISBN-13: 978-1-59669-253-4	ISBN-13: 978-1-59669-252-7

Available in bookstores everywhere

For information about these books or any New Hope product,
visit www.newhopepublishers.com.